MCWP 3-37

MAGTF Nuclear, Biological, and Chemical Defense Operations

U.S. Marine Corps

PCN 143 000010 00

Reviewed and approved this date:

BY DIRECTION OF THE COMMANDANT OF THE MARINE CORPS

J. E. Rhodes

J. E. RHODES
Lieutenant General, U.S. Marine Corps
Commanding General
Marine Corps Combat Development Command

DISTRIBUTION: 143 000010 00

DEPARTMENT OF THE NAVY
Headquarters United States Marine Corps
Washington, DC 20380-1775

21 September 1998

FOREWORD

Marine Corps Warfighting Publication (MCWP) 3-37, *MAGTF Nuclear, Biological, and Chemical Defense Operations*, addresses the planning and execution of NBC defense operations within the Marine air-ground task force (MAGTF). It sets forth the doctrinal foundation for all subsequent Marine Corps publications on nuclear, biological, and chemical (NBC) defense. This publication is designed for commanders, their staffs, and the individual Marine responsible for the planning, execution, and, ultimately, operations of amphibious and expeditionary operations conducted in an NBC environment. MCWP 3-37 also identifies responsibilities and provides MAGTF NBC guidance for organizational structure, personnel functions, and command and staff relationships.

Standardization Agreement (STANAG) 2150, *NATO Standards of Proficiency for NBC Defense*, has been implemented in this publication.

MCWP 3-37 supersedes Operational Handbook (OH) 11, *MAGTF Nuclear, Chemical, and Defensive Biological Operations*, dated 18 January 1991.

MAGTF Nuclear, Biological, and Chemical Defense Operations

Table of Contents

Chapter 4   Passive and Active NBC Planning Measures

Chapter 5   NBC Defense Training

Appendices

Notes

Glossary

References and Related Publications

Chapter 1

The Threat

"We have the power to knock any society out of the Twentieth Century."[1]

—Robert S. McNamara

Despite worldwide efforts to contain the spread of technologies associated with nuclear, biological, and chemical (NBC) warfare, countries desiring to have a weapon of mass destruction (WMD) have found ways to initiate WMD programs. There are three recognized conditions that determine if a country is capable of initiating a WMD program. The country has the—

- Ability to obtain or produce a weapons-grade nuclear material, a biological agent, or a chemical agent.
- Ability to make the material or agent into a weapon or device.
- Ability to deliver the weapon or device.

As more countries obtain these capabilities, the future use of WMD by a threat country to counter the capabilities of the Marine air-ground task force (MAGTF) is increasingly likely. Marine Corps Intelligence Activity (MCIA) publication 1586-001-97, *Marine Corps Midrange Threat Estimate—1997–2007: Finding Order in Chaos (U)*, identifies countries (listed in table 1-1) that have or can field a WMD program.[2] Despite treaties that ban NBC weapons, many of these countries have researched the use of one or a combination of these weapons as a WMD.

Table 1-1: Countries of Concern to the Marine Corps

Afghanistan	Indonesia	Philippines
Algeria	Iran	Russia
Angola	Iraq	Rwanda
Bangladesh	Israel	Somalia
Bosnia	North Korea	Sudan
Burundi	Liberia	Syria
China	Libya	Taiwan
Cuba	Mozamique	Turkey
Ethiopia	Niger	Vietnam
Haiti	Nigeria	Yugoslavia
India	Peru	Zaire

Nuclear Threat

The seven admitted nuclear powers are France, India, People's Republic of China, Pakistan, Russia, the United Kingdom, and the United States. These countries have demonstrated that they possess a nuclear capability. In addition, Iran, Iraq, Israel, Libya, and North Korea have declared their intent to obtain, a nuclear weapons capability.

The potential use of a nuclear weapon within a regional or limited conflict poses a substantial threat to the MAGTF. Sufficient controls have not been emplaced to stop the proliferation of nuclear weapons technology, materials, and delivery systems. The likelihood of an emerging nuclear nation being able to develop a large-yield nuclear weapon is remote. However, the development of low-yield, multi-kiloton devices and limited-range delivery systems is probable. The demise of the former Soviet Union greatly diminished the threat of an intercontinental exchange of nuclear weapons, but the potential use of small tactical nuclear devices in regional conflicts has increased due to the continuing spread of nuclear technology and materials.

Biological Threat

Throughout the history of warfare, disease has caused more casualties than weapons. Influenza, cholera, yellow fever, plague, malaria, and infections have always been a part of military campaigns. As a result of poor vector control (i.e., rats, mosquitoes, fleas) or hygiene, biological warfare is the least controllable form of WMD. Many technologies associated with peaceful biological research are also applicable to the development of biological warfare agents. The ability to conduct legitimate research and develop biological warfare technologies simultaneously makes proliferation control difficult. Egypt, Iran, Iraq, Libya, North Korea, People's Republic of China, Russia, and Syria are some of the countries that have the potential to develop biological programs. As noted before, many of these same countries are on the Marine Corps' list of countries of concern.

The most common biological agents that may be expected are anthrax, botulinum, cholera, and plague. Some of the more exotic and potentially dangerous biological warfare agents are algae toxins, altered microbes, bioregulators, brucellosis, encephalitis, glanders, hemorrhagic fever, mycotoxins (yellow rain), peptice ionophores, Q fever, ricin, saxitoxin, smallpox, staphylococcal enterotoxins, tetrodotoxin, tularemia, and venom toxins.

The threat of naturally occurring disease, particularly in Third World countries, is always of concern to the warfighter. The deliberate use of biological agents as a weapon directed against Marines is an added threat that the MAGTF must be prepared to address.

Chemical Threat

Due to the relative ease of production, chemical agents are the most likely form of WMD to be encountered. The use of chemical warfare has a history that spans the 20th century. The following list, which is not inclusive, identifies conflicts in which chemical weapons were used:

World War I	1915–1918
Italy-Ethiopia	1935–1936
Japan-China	1935–1944
Egypt-Yemen	1963–1967
Southeast Asia	1970s
USSR-Afghanistan	1980s
China-Vietnam	1980s
Iran-Iraq	1983–1988
Iraq-Kurds	1990s

It is estimated that chemical agents are stockpiled or are under development in 20 to 25 countries. They cover the entire spectrum of blister, blood, incapacitant, and nerve agents. The most common are sulfur mustard-H (blister), tabun-GA (nerve), sarin-GB (nerve), soman-GF (nerve), and VX (nerve).

Access to chemicals for legitimate use in industry and agriculture increases the difficulty of controlling the proliferation of chemical warfare agents. One major proliferation control involves the close monitoring of precursor chemicals; however, a likely trend is that threat countries and terrorists interested in developing WMD will attempt to circumvent monitoring processes.

Many of the same countries associated with a nuclear or biological program have established, or are seeking to establish, chemical weapons programs. Egypt, France, Iran, Libya, Iraq, People's Republic of China, Syria, Russia, and many of the countries belonging to the former Warsaw Pact (Bulgaria, Czech Republic, Poland, Romania, Slovakia, and the former Yugoslav republics) have, or are suspected of having, chemical weapons programs. Table 1-1 includes many of these countries. Obviously, the use of chemical warfare, particularly in regional conflicts, poses a significant threat to MAGTF operations.

Chapter 2

Organization and Responsibilities

"No military or naval force, in war, can accomplish any-thing worthwhile unless there is back of it the work of an efficient, loyal, and devoted staff."[1]
> —Lieutenant General Hunter Liggett, USA

Both the size and composition of a MAGTF and an NBC unit depend on mission, enemy, terrain and weather, troops and support available-time available (METT-T). To conduct NBC defense effectively, the force requires a clear understanding of the mission, command relationships, and the available resources. Since the Marine Corps has a limited number of military occupational speciality (MOS)-qualified NBC specialists (MOS 5702 and MOS 5711), these specialists are placed where they will have the greatest impact on overall mission accomplishment. This means that positions on most NBC teams will not be filled with NBC specialists. Therefore, the success of an NBC team relies on the competency of the individual Marine. Individual Marines must hone their individual NBC skills and their understanding of NBC defense operations. Their responses to NBC defense operations must become conditioned responses. Based on this information, the MAGTF commander considers the following while forming the MAGTF's NBC defense:

- All NBC personnel and equipment organic to the units assigned to, or under the operational control (OPCON) of, the MAGTF.

- Additional NBC equipment and personnel available from senior agencies (e.g., joint task force).

- The MAGTF's command and support relationships.

- The availability of NBC specialists (MOS 5702 and MOS 5711 personnel).

All echelons of command must supervise and reinforce the NBC defense efforts of subordinate elements. Each commander in a MAGTF must prepare and implement NBC defense measures while also ensuring that their subordinates can operate in a NBC environment. To provide adequate defense, the MAGTF commander organizes NBC defense assets as described on pages 2-4 through 2-16. Units at all levels must be capable of performing the following essential operations:

- Detecting and identifying NBC agents and materials.

- Warning of and reporting NBC attacks and hazards.

- Performing individual and collective protection measures.

- Decontaminating personnel, equipment, and terrain as required.

- Administering first aid and following unit medical operations and exposure guidance.

Regardless of the unit's size or mission, principles essential to NBC defense remain constant; only the scope will vary. The following principles help to determine the structure of effective NBC teams and units:

- The lowest level of organization required to function as an independent unit must possess the capability to survive and accomplish specialized tasks in an NBC environment.

- Higher units or formations must also be capable of accomplishing their own mission as well as supporting subordinate units if required.

- Specific personnel must be designated and trained for specific NBC defense responsibilities.

NBC teams and units are structured to support subordinate commanders as much as possible while drawing as little as possible from the supported commanders' assets. For example, a battalion headquarters maintains some level of NBC decontamination capability. This may be in the form of personnel support or equipment support. A battalion commander can reinforce the decontamination efforts of one subordinate commander by dispatching part of the headquarters, the headquarters and service (H&S) company decontamination team, or equipment assets rather than using the decontamination team(s) of another line company unit. If a line company commander loses the assigned decontamination team, the commander loses the only personnel used to perform primary NBC duties and capabilities (immediate decontamination).

The framework for effective NBC defense operations is in place once the MAGTF is fully deployed. Additional NBC defense organizations can be created using appropriate command and support relationships. The creation of additional NBC defense organizations should not change the defense mission of NBC organizations already in existence. Consideration should be given to the demand or reservoirs of available assets before any additional NBC defense organizations are created.

Control Centers

The NBC control center (see fig. 2-1 on page 2-4) forms the hub for all NBC defense operations. The control center monitors and coordinates all NBC defense operations. It is also responsible for collecting, collating, analyzing, and disseminating all NBC-related information. NBC information may come from many different agencies or units. As a general rule, NBC information gathering focuses on early warning of NBC attacks, locations of contaminated areas, decontamination sites, and routes from contaminated areas to decontamination sites.

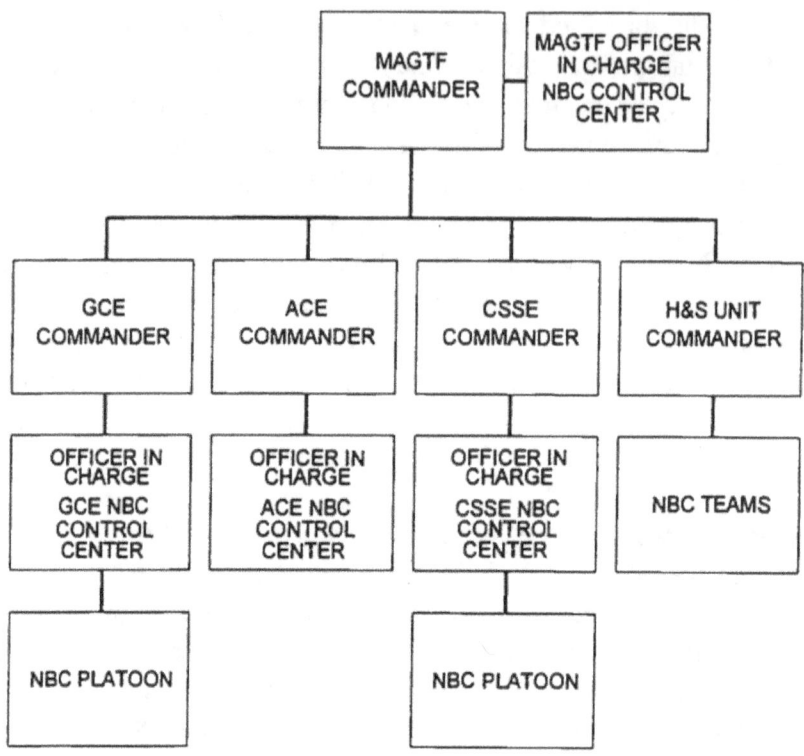

Figure 2-1. NBC Control Centers.

Command Element

The command element coordinates reconnaissance/survey operations, coordinates surveillance/monitoring operations, and coordinates and monitors decontamination operations. It maintains close coordination with all intelligence assets in order to exchange NBC reconnaissance/survey intelligence. The command element is also responsible for collecting, collating, analyzing, and disseminating surveillance/monitoring information.

Headquarters and service unit's NBC defense teams conduct NBC defense operations for the command element.

Many different units on the battlefield will be in a position to report NBC activity; therefore, the command element must be prepared to establish an NBC control center that is capable of continuous operations. An NBC control center cannot be established with only the NBC officer and NBC specialists assigned to the command element. Augmentation is required. Units that are not committed may provide additional NBC personnel to the command element in order to augment the NBC control center.

Ground Combat Element

The ground combat element (GCE) company and battalion teams organize as elements of their respective units. Since the threat of an NBC attack is equal to all ground combat units, the GCE commander normally leaves all NBC assets with the parent organization. The division NBC platoon is placed either in a general or direct support role based on the NBC threat and the ability to facilitate future operations.

If augmentation is required, the officer in charge of the GCE NBC control center coordinates with the officer in charge of the higher headquarters NBC control center. Augmentation provided is based on assets available and operational priorities.

Marine Division

The division G-3 section contains the NBC section. Personnel required to staff an NBC control center are drawn from this section. In addition to performing control center functions at the division level, NBC personnel supervise overall NBC operations planning, organization, and readiness of subordinate units. Although limited in its capability, this section also can perform NBC reconnaissance.

The division NBC section also provides the nucleus for a reinforced NBC platoon. This unit, with personnel from division elements, combat engineers, and motor transport augmentation, forms an NBC defense organization that can support a division's decontamination operation and support the NBC readiness of the MAGTF's GCE.

A further combination of personnel and equipment from the combat engineer battalion, hygiene equipment section, and the division NBC platoon creates a provisional unit that possesses increased decontamination capabilities. If required, this provisional unit is task-organized to provide support to the GCE.

Regiment

The regiment's NBC defense needs are met with as little rearrangement of existing personnel and equipment as possible. The regimental commander assigns the NBC officer as the officer in charge and task-organizes organic assets. If additional assistance is required, the regimental commander requests reinforcement from higher headquarters.

NBC Officer and NBC Noncommissioned Officer

Infantry and artillery regiments are staffed with an NBC officer (MOS 5702) to assist the commander and the staff in NBC defense operations. An NBC specialist (MOS 5711) is assigned to assist the NBC officer. Other noncommissioned officers (NCOs) may be assigned the responsibilities of NBC NCOs as additional duties.

NBC Section

Infantry regiments have assigned NBC specialists by table of organization (T/O). The composition and duties of the NBC control center team parallel those of the battalion NBC organization discussed below. However, the information processed at this level is more voluminous and broader in scope.

Decontamination Capability

The regiment does not maintain a standing decontamination team. NBC personnel of the regiment coordinate and supervise the decontamination efforts within the regiment. The operational decontamination of regimental headquarters is performed by the regimental headquarters company decontamination team or other designated personnel.

Battalions

A unit's NBC defense needs are met with as little rearrangement of existing personnel and equipment as possible. Consolidation of NBC defense assets under the cognizance of the battalion NBC officer is neither the recommended nor the preferred method of supporting the battalion's NBC defense requirements. The battalion NBC officer advises the commander and coordinates the efforts, but the battalion NBC officer does not exercise command authority.

NBC Officer and NBC NCO

Battalions are authorized an NBC specialist (MOS 5711) by T/O, and, in some cases, they are authorized an NBC officer (MOS 5702). These personnel are assigned to the S-3 section. If an NBC officer (MOS 5702) is not available to occupy these T/O billets, an officer is assigned the duties of NBC officer as an additional duty. The battalion NBC officer should attend a command level NBC defense course. Each battalion must ensure that the NBC officer and NBC NCO are trained and assigned as needed.

NBC Control Center

The GCE NBC control center collects, evaluates, collates, and disseminates information concerning friendly and enemy NBC operations to the commander, his staff, higher headquarters, subordinate units, and supporting units. Specifically, the GCE NBC control center—

- Plans the employment of NBC detectors and sensors.
- Disseminates tasks of the monitor/survey teams.
- Disseminates overall unit NBC defense guidance.
- Coordinates troop safety considerations when friendly NBC operations are planned.
- Performs the computations needed to convert basic NBC information into the required form.
- Plots and displays NBC information.
- Evaluates NBC information.
- Disseminates NBC information.

Each battalion commander organizes and trains a GCE NBC control center team. The GCE NBC control center is normally located within the combat operations center (COC). This facilitates close coordination with the operations section, intelligence section, and the fire support coordination center (FSCC).

Commanders and their staffs use the information collected and processed by the GCE NBC control center team to assist them in their decisionmaking process. This information influences the tactical employment of monitor/survey teams and the conduct of operations based on the existing level of contamination.

Decontamination Capability

Generally, a battalion does not maintain a standing decontamination team. Immediate decontamination is normally performed by company decontamination teams, although decontamination efforts can be a coordinated effort that uses battalion headquarters and company equipment assets and teams.

As the need for decontamination operations increases, the battalion NBC officer's mission is to coordinate the support requirements of subordinate commanders and enhance their ability to perform their mission. The battalion NBC standing operating procedures (SOP) structures the NBC defense organization to reinforce subordinate unit capabilities and to avoid stripping them of their ability to perform decontamination operations. The inclination to consolidate NBC defense assets at the battalion level must be avoided. Instead, the battalion NBC SOP should address training and organizing a maximum number of personnel, from the combat service support (CSS) elements of the battalion, in NBC decontamination operations. The battalion NBC officer coordinates the employment of CSS NBC personnel when reinforcing subordinate unit decontamination operations. Additional support, if required, is requested from the next higher headquarters. If assets organic to the regiment cannot be provided, the request for assistance is forwarded to the next higher headquarters.

Monitor/Survey Capability

To meet the battalion's surveillance requirements, the battalion commander normally tasks subordinate unit monitor/survey teams with surveillance and monitoring responsibilities. If this is impractical, part or all of the company monitor/survey teams may be consolidated, and the battalion NBC officer is placed in charge of the teams. Consolidation of NBC assets is the exception rather than the rule for meeting the needs of battalion NBC defense. Only under extreme circumstances should consolidation of assets be considered. Senior commanders can also assign NBC teams to, or place NBC teams in support of, the battalion commander.

Companies

Company commanders organize and train NBC defense team(s) and other NBC personnel according to unit SOPs and directives issued from higher headquarters. During actual NBC operations, NBC-trained personnel can be assigned to full-time NBC defense duties. A generic organization consists of several monitor/survey teams and a decontamination team. Detailed procedures and techniques on the composition of and requirements for NBC defense teams are contained in the following allied tactical publication (ATP), U.S. Army field manuals (FMs), Fleet Marine Force manuals (FMFMs), Marine Corps warfighting publication (MCWP), naval medical (NAVMED) publication, and Air Force joint manual (AFJMAN):

- ATP 45, *Reporting Nuclear Detonations, Biological and Chemical Attacks, and Predicting and Warning of Associated Hazards and Hazard Areas.*

- FM 3-3-1/FMFM 11-18, *Nuclear Contamination Avoidance.*

- FM 3-4/FMFM 11-9, *NBC Protection.*

- FM 3-5/FMFM 11-10, *NBC Decontamination.*

- FM 3-7/MCRP 3-37A, *NBC Field Handbook.*

- FM 3-100/MCWP 3-3.7.1, *Chemical Operations, Principles, and Fundamentals.*

- FM 8-285/NAVMED P-5041/AFJMAN 44-149/FMFM 11-11, *Treatment of Chemical Casualties and Conventional Military Chemical Injuries.*

Equipment

Companies have chemical agent detector kits, radiological detection equipment, and other protective and decontamination material listed in their tables of equipment (T/Es). NBC defense equipment, though authorized in company unit T/Es, is usually maintained under the centralized control of the battalion or group NBC officer for accountability purposes.

Sentries and Guards. During NBC operations, sentries and guards have the additional duties of initiating the chemical attack alarm and participating in other chemical defense activities. Each sentry must know how to sound the alarm to alert unit personnel to a chemical, biological, or radiological hazard.

NBC Defense Team Personnel. The company-level NBC defense team consists of organic personnel assigned the additional duty of NBC defense. Higher headquarters SOPs dictate the team's exact composition. Generally, a company NBC defense team consists of:

- The NBC officer who supervises NBC defense activities.
- The NBC NCO who assists the NBC officer.
- Personnel trained to decontaminate unit equipment and supplies.
- Trained monitors or operators to use radiac meters and chemical detection kits as rated by unit T/Es.
- Ground survey parties for survey meters authorized by T/E. At a minimum, the survey party consists of qualified ground surveyors, drivers, radio operators, and security personnel as required.

NBC Defense Team Capabilities

The company NBC defense team(s) must be able to—

- Conduct NBC reconnaissance.
- Recognize NBC attacks and understand unit procedures to implement warnings.
- Detect chemical and biological agents and radiological hazards.
- Operate and perform operator's maintenance on NBC detection and sampling equipment.
- Conduct NBC sampling surveys.
- Collect samples of suspected contamination and forward to higher headquarters.

- Mark contaminated areas, equipment, and supplies with standard marking signs.

- Provide data for compilation of NBC reports.

- Perform monitor/survey functions.

- Operate and perform operator's maintenance on NBC monitoring equipment.

- Conduct NBC monitoring operations.

- Monitor effectiveness of decontamination measures.

- Provide data for completion of NBC reports.

- Perform decontamination.

Aviation Combat Element

The current structure of the Marine aircraft wing (MAW) includes all the NBC officers and specialists required to sustain foreseeable NBC defense operations. Additional support is requested through the command element NBC control center.

Marine Aircraft Wing Headquarters

The MAW G-3 section contains the NBC personnel required to staff an aviation combat element (ACE) NBC control center. This center is normally located in the tactical air command center. These personnel perform overall NBC defense planning, organization, and readiness for their units.

The MAW does not have a specialized NBC unit at the headquarters level. However, the organization of NBC specialists and the NBC tasks assigned to various units ensure there is a coordinated effort to accomplish all NBC defense missions.

Marine Aircraft Group

The Marine aircraft group (MAG) headquarters consists of one NBC officer (MOS 5702) and several NBC specialists (MOS 5711). The MAG headquarters is the lowest MAW level with an NBC specialist (with the exception of the Marine wing support squadron [MWSS]). When attached to subordinate units, MAG NBC personnel provide guidance on NBC matters and coordinate with the MWSS concerning all aspects of operational decontamination, contamination control, and NBC reconnaissance.

Squadron/Battalion

NBC Officer and NBC NCO

NBC defense specialists are normally consolidated at the MAG level (except for the MWSS). This allows for centralized control of the maintenance of equipment, NBC warning and reporting, and NBC training. Although NBC specialists are not located at all levels, all squadrons are still required to—

- Maintain individual and unit NBC defense equipment. This includes maintenance, calibration, distribution, and requisition.
- Ensure that each equipment or vehicle operator, weapons crewman, and aircraft crewman can perform spot decontamination of their equipment, vehicle, or aircraft.

ACE NBC Control Center Team

Although MAW squadrons and battalions are not required to establish an ACE NBC control center team, they must be prepared to submit to higher headquarters NBC 1 and 4 reports. They also must be capable of analyzing and assessing NBC 2, 3, and 5 reports (see MCRP 3-37A, *NBC Field Handbook*) in order to take appropriate actions. Therefore, if a squadron is in support of a MAGTF as the aviation combat element, the requirement for manning a control center would best be managed by the MAGTF headquarters. The MAGTF headquarters has sufficient personnel to provide the ACE commander with information concerning friendly and enemy NBC operations. If required, the MWSS provides an NBC defense control center to the ACE.

Decontamination Capability

Each squadron will be capable of performing immediate and operational decontamination of its personnel and equipment. If thorough decontamination operations are necessary, each squadron should be prepared to augment the MWSS with extra personnel to facilitate their support of squadron decontamination efforts.

Monitor/Survey Capability

If directed, each squadron will provide personnel to the MWSS in support of airfield monitor/survey team operations.

Marine Wing Support Squadron

The MWSS has an NBC defense section that consists of 9 enlisted personnel for a fixed-wing support squadron and 10 enlisted personnel for a rotary-wing support squadron. The MWSS NBC defense section has a decontamination station supervisor for each type of detailed decontamination. It also has a contamination control supervisor and an NBC control center that may be attached to the ACE. It may be necessary to obtain augmentation from the other squadrons within the group in order to fully staff the control center.

Combat Service Support Element

Combat service support element (CSSE) battalions possess the equipment and personnel required to perform NBC defense operations. The NBC decontamination company is organized and attached to the CSSE command element based on the NBC threat.

Force Service Support Group Headquarters

The force service support group (FSSG) G-3 section contains an NBC defense platoon consisting of 2 NBC officers and 36 NBC specialists. Elements of this platoon are used to—

- Form the CSSE NBC control center.

- Coordinate, evaluate, and, if necessary, augment any NBC defense operations conducted within the FSSG area of responsibility.

- Provide the nucleus of a reinforced platoon or provisional unit to support MAGTF operations with deliberate decontamination support as directed by the MAGTF command element.

Decontamination Capability

The motor transport battalion has transport assets that can support the NBC unit. The FSSG commander can augment the NBC platoon with engineers and with other assets from the FSSG to form a reinforced platoon or provisional unit. Engineer officers and enlisted hygiene equipment operators from the shower unit of the engineer support battalion can be trained in NBC decontamination operations. In addition to thorough decontamination operations, the reinforced platoon or unit can provide—

- Shower operations.

- Water purification.

- Water point and NBC reconnaissance.

- Water storage.

- Desalinization operations.

- Generator, air-conditioning, and refrigeration maintenance.

- Collective protection shelter construction.

- Thorough decontamination operations.

Staff Responsibilities in NBC Operations

As a staff officer, the MAGTF NBC officer has no authority over subordinate commanders. NBC defense is part of all operations and NBC defense operations are often conducted with the same assets that perform other tasks assigned to subordinate commanders. Therefore, care must be taken when delegating authority to NBC officers to ensure that their instructions and those of the commander and operations officer do not conflict.

Timeliness, accuracy, and efficiency of MAGTF command and staff actions in an NBC environment depend on the staff's state of preparedness. Staff officers need to understand the characteristics and effects of NBC weapons as they relate to the conduct of specific warfighting functions. Staff considerations for NBC warfare must become a routine concern in the planning and training phases of a MAGTF's continuous preparation for combat operations. Effective staff support in an NBC environment is facilitated by—

- Knowledge of general and special staff functions.

- Knowledge of staff planning and command and staff NBC considerations.

- Knowledge of NBC weapons, effects, and personnel and material responses.

To effectively defend against an NBC attack, commanders and staff officers require a general knowledge of the characteristics, effects, and concept for employment and defense against NBC munitions. The technical knowledge and skills required for NBC defense are provided by personnel especially trained for NBC duties. These specialists form the nucleus (NBC section) for NBC staff functions within the MAGTF. During NBC operations, these sections organize into NBC control centers. NBC control centers are formed at all echelons of command down to the battalion level. The NBC officer, under the cognizance of the G-3/S-3, supervises the NBC control center and all NBC operations. At each echelon of command, the NBC officer/NCO assists and makes recommendations to the appropriate staff officer.

Assistant Chief of Staff, G-1/S-1

The G-1/S-1—

- Prepares and maintains NBC casualty records, reports, and unit radiation dosage records in coordination with the medical officer and NBC officer/NCO.

- Coordinates radiation exposure status of subordinate organizations with the G-3/S-3 and medical officer.

- Incorporates contamination considerations.

- Determines straggler control measures.

- Supervises graves registration.

- Coordinates with the NBC officer for the handling of prisoners of war (POWs) in order to provide NBC protective equipment and self-decontamination operations as specified in current international agreements and treaties.

- Coordinates with the G-3/S-3 for the appropriate priority/ assignment of personnel to NBC billets.

Assistant Chief of Staff, G-2/S-2

The G-2/S-2—

- Supervises the production and dissemination of intelligence in the following areas:

  - Enemy NBC capabilities including production capabilities, weapons, and delivery systems.

  - Enemy NBC defense equipment and training status.

  - Enemy intent to use NBC weapons.

- Identifies and locates targets appropriate for nuclear attack.

- Initiates activities that degrade and counter the enemy's ability to acquire targets for NBC attack.

- Recommends NBC reconnaissance of routes and areas.

Assistant Chief of Staff, G-3/S-3

The G-3/S-3—

- Prepares operation plans, orders, appendices, and annexes in accordance with the commander's guidance for NBC operations.

- Considers the NBC threat when determining the general location of the command post.

- Plans and coordinates NBC defense training and inspections.

- Reviews and updates NBC defense SOPs as well as training SOPs.

- Prepares and supervises the NBC training program.

- Supervises training of NBC monitor/survey teams, decontamination teams, and NBC control center personnel.

- Inspects subordinate units' NBC equipment.

- Activates the NBC control center and coordinates its activities.

- Prepares and disseminates friendly force hazard predictions, minimum mission oriented protective posture (MOPP) recommendations, and effective downwind messages to subordinate units.

- Recommends required units, personnel, and equipment to conduct radiological/chemical surveys.

- Forwards NBC reports and enemy NBC attack alerts to higher, subordinate, and adjacent units or headquarters.

- Directs and supervises chemical detection, biological sampling, and radiological monitor/survey operations and reports within the unit.

- Ensures the preparation and promulgation of troop safety information.

Assistant Chief of Staff, G-4/S-4

The G-4/S-4—

- Disperses logistic support facilities to reduce vulnerability to NBC weapons.

- Plans for increased transportation requirements due to the dispersion of units, increased demand for NBC replacement equipment, and decontamination logistic requirements.

- Ensures availability of NBC defense equipment.

- Supervises maintenance of NBC defense equipment.

- Develops plans to transport increased numbers of uncontaminated and contaminated casualties.

- Plans for large-scale, thorough decontamination operations in response to an NBC attack.

- Prepares plans for and, when directed, supervises the construction and/or use of personnel shelters, decontamination sites, emergency power plants, and laundry facilities.

- Receives recommendations from the NBC officer or NCO on NBC equipment and supply requirements.

- Receives NBC equipment and supply request information from the NBC officer or NCO and effectively ensures distribution.

- Supervises installation and establishment of collective protection facilities as recommended by the NBC officer or NCO.

Medical Officer

The medical officer—

- Prescribes treatment procedures for NBC casualties.

- Ensures that facilities for treatment of NBC casualties are available.

- Supervises the inspection of food and water supplies for signs of contamination.

- Coordinates with the NBC control center to monitor and evaluate a subordinate unit's nuclear radiation exposure history.

- Advises the commander and G-3/S-3 on the impact of a unit's additional exposure.

- Makes recommendations to prevent, and takes actions to detect, contamination of food and water supplies.

- Coordinates the collection and processing of all biological samples with the unit NBC defense officer.

- Oversees periodic monitoring of all individual health records to ensure up-to-date immunization of all personnel against potential biological agents.

- Verifies that personnel requiring optical inserts have them.

- Ensures the training of medical personnel in the treatment of NBC casualties.

- Coordinates the training of Marines to identify NBC symptoms.

- Provides first aid response in conjunction with the G-3/S-3.

- Coordinates, with the G-4/S-4, the procurement and distribution of all medical supplies required for the treatment of NBC casualties.

- Develops plans, in coordination with the G-4/S-4, for the handling and movement of contaminated casualties.

- Plans and supervises medical treatment of POWs and civilian internees and detainees that may have been exposed to NBC agents.

- Assists the G-1/S-1 in maintaining radiation exposure records.

- Maintains and distributes, in coordination with the NBC officer or NCO, information on NBC antidotes.

- Coordinates with the NBC officer or NCO to determine the requirements for medical personnel in casualty decontamination.

Engineer Officer

The engineer officer—

- Provides engineer technical expertise in the decontamination of engineer equipment.

- Coordinates, with the G-4/S-4, NBC officer, and appropriate construction units, the building of thorough decontamination sites. Primary emphasis is on the utilization of existing structures.

- Plans for construction of fortifications, installations, and facilities that provide maximum protection against NBC weapons.

- Prepares plans for emergency tasks. This includes water decontamination and restoration of tactical facilities.

- Recommends traffic regulations for routes of communication. Recommendations must address physical and contamination conditions.

- Coordinates well-drilling operations with naval construction battalions.

- Maintains "B" table of authorized material control number (TAMCN) NBC decontamination equipment.

Motor Transport Officer

The motor transport officer—

- Assists in the decontamination of motor transport equipment.

- Coordinates with the G-4/S-4 for the mass evacuation of personnel and material under NBC conditions.

- Coordinates with the G-4/S-4 and NBC officer for the possible use of maintenance facilities as decontamination sites.

Supply Officer

The supply officer—

- Coordinates, with the G-4/S-4, the acquisition, storage, control, issue, security, recovery, supervision, and redistribution of all NBC equipment and supplies.

- Provides advice and supervises NBC supply procedures. This includes property accountability and responsibility.

Assistant Chief of Staff, G-6/S-6

The G-6/S-6—

- Supervises maintenance of radiac equipment in accordance with appropriate technical instructions.

- Provides a communications-electronics annex to operational orders/plans. This includes appropriate net utilization for NBC traffic if required.

- Provides communications for NBC teams directly under the control of the headquarters.

- Prepares special communications plans for mass casualty evacuation.

- Plans to counter the effect of electromagnetic pulse on communication equipment.

Division Artillery Officer

The division artillery officer—

- Coordinates with supporting artillery commander and/or meteorological detachment to provide meteorological data for use in fallout prediction.

- Coordinates the requirement for chemical downwind messages.

NBC Defense Officer

The duties and responsibilities of Marine Corps forces unit NBC officers are determined by the unit level of assignment. In the broadest terms, their primary concern is the establishment of passive NBC defensive measures.

Division, Wing, FSSG, and MAGTF Command Elements

These unit NBC officers—

- Advise the commander on NBC defense readiness.

- Advise the commander on operational exposure guidance.

- Prepare the NBC defense plans, orders, and instructions necessary to implement the commander's policies. This includes SOPs for NBC defense, NBC orders and annexes, and NBC inspections.

- Determine and recommend requirements for NBC supplies and equipment.

- Estimate personnel, equipment, and supply requirements to support the NBC appendix of the operation order.

- Coordinate and develop NBC defense training exercises.

- Evaluate unit NBC defense readiness.

- Supervise operation of the NBC control center.

- Conduct and supervise NBC equipment inspections.

- Provide recommendations for the training of the command and for the training of NBC specialists. This includes formal school quotas.

- Provide technical assistance in the examination of captured NBC equipment.

- Plan and make recommendations for decontamination functions.

- Perform other duties as directed.

Regiment, Group, and Battalion

These unit NBC officers—

- Provide information (in conjunction with the G-2/S-2) concerning NBC organization, weapons, equipment, and techniques indicative of enemy preparations for an NBC attack.

- Provide information (in conjunction with the G-2/S-2) concerning the effects of terrain and weather on enemy or friendly employment of NBC agents.

- Determine NBC reconnaissance (in conjunction with the G-2/S-2) required in areas or routes intended for use by friendly troops.

- Plan NBC monitor/survey operations within the unit's area of operation.

- Interpret radiological information (fallout prediction, actual fallout, and monitor information).

- Appraise tactical significance of residual radiation areas.

- Coordinate with the medical officer to determine radiation effects on personnel.

- Interpret chemical information (chemical prediction and monitor/survey data).

- Coordinate the unit NBC defense training program.

- Plan for immediate and operational decontamination of personnel and equipment.

- Supervise the procurement, issue, installation, and maintenance of unit NBC equipment.

- Supervise the operation of the NBC control center.

- Advise assignment of NBC-trained personnel.

- Monitor employment of NBC defense teams.

- Notify commanders if contaminated areas are within the area of operation.

- Supervise training and activities of the NBC specialist.

- Advise subordinate commander.

Company, Battery, and Squadron

At the company, battery, and squadron levels, NBC responsibilities are usually assigned as an additional duty. These unit NBC officers—

- Train unit-level individuals in the effective use of individual NBC protective items.

- Supervise company, battery, and squadron monitoring/survey operations.

- Supervise NBC reconnaissance of routes and areas to be occupied.

- Supervise the preparation of NBC 1 and 4 reports.

- Maintain company, battery, and squadron radiation dosage records.

- Advise the battalion or group NBC officer on the conduct of integrated NBC training within the company, battery, or squadron training program.

- Assist in first aid or evacuation of NBC casualties.

- Supervise basic skills and immediate decontamination of personnel and equipment.

- Supervise the training of NBC techniques and procedures; i.e., unmasking procedures and crossing of contaminated area.

- Supervise the marking of contaminated areas.

- Supervise the training and activities of the NBC NCO.

NBC Defense Specialist

NBC specialist billets are incorporated into the Marine Corps T/O (listed as NBC NCOs) at levels of the command down to the battalion level. The NBC specialist, like the NBC officer, is a member of the G-3/S-3 section. The specialist maintains the unit's NBC defense equipment, trains Marines in NBC defense measures and protection, and advises the unit NBC officer on all NBC defense matters. Specific training standards are listed in Marine Corps Order (MCO) 1510.71A, *Individual Training Standards (ITS) System for NBC Defense Specialists, MOS 5711; and for NBC Officers, MOS 5702*. The duties of the NBC specialist, like those of the NBC officer, vary with the level of command. The NBC specialist should be prepared to assist the NBC officer.

Division, Wing, FSSG, and MAGTF Command Elements

NBC defense specialists in these organizations—

- Assist the NBC officer in the execution of duties.

- Assist the NBC officer in ensuring that NBC SOPs are up-to-date and effectively promulgated.

- Maintain or assist in maintaining NBC publications.

- Recommend unit NBC training requirements.

- Provide direct supervision to the administration of the NBC control center.

- Plan NBC monitor/survey operations.

- Prepare voice Joint Interoperability of Tactical Command and Control Systems (JINTACCS) messages for NBC reports.

Regiment, Group, and Battalion

NBC defense specialists in these organizations—

- Assist the NBC officer in the execution of duties.

- Inspect or assist in the inspection of NBC equipment for serviceability.

- Assist the NBC officer in ensuring that NBC SOPs are up-to-date and effectively promulgated.

- Maintain or assist in maintaining NBC equipment.

- Conduct sizing and fitting of protective masks.

- Supervise monitor/survey operations.

- Provide direct supervision of the NBC control center.

- Assist in organizing and training of NBC teams.

- Establish or assist in establishing an NBC maintenance program.

- Maintain or assist in maintaining NBC publications.
- Establish or assist in establishing an effective NBC equipment warehousing and supply program.

Company, Battery, and Squadron

NBC defense specialists in these organizations—

- Supervise unit-level personnel and equipment decontamination.
- Organize and train NBC teams.
- Assist the unit NBC NCO by ensuring that NBC equipment is turned in upon completion of training or as required for conducting maintenance and serviceability inspections.
- Assist and monitor all required individual training.

Chapter 3

Combat Service Support in an NBC Environment

"Every unit that is not supported is a defeated unit."[1]
—Maurice de Saxe

The task organization of MAGTF elements determines CSS relationships in an NBC environment. MAGTF CSS requirements are tailored to provide support beyond that which is organic to subordinate elements. Combat service support in an NBC environment is more difficult. Therefore, it is critical that NBC CSS requirements be completely addressed during planning to ensure successful mission accomplishment. NBC mass destruction capabilities can severely drain a CSS system. Supplies and equipment can be lost because of destruction or contamination. Decontamination of equipment prior to repair increases maintenance time. Issue and exchange of protective clothing and equipment create logistic overloads. Water requirements increase due to increased consumption by individual Marines and increased use in medical and decontamination operations. Medical services are heavily burdened as a new category of injury is introduced to the battlefield. Mass casualty evacuation becomes more likely and can severely tax an already burdened transportation system.

The threat of enemy NBC attack significantly changes the concept of tactical operations and the logistical support of a military force. Since it is impossible to predict combat losses in an NBC environment, logistical planners must plan for worst case scenarios to ensure logistic sustainability of MAGTF operations and successful mission accomplishment. Therefore, assessing enemy capability and intent becomes essential to NBC defense planning and employment. Modifying standard logistic procedures is required to reduce the risk of loss from NBC attack and to compensate for expected losses.

Supply

NBC operations require more supplies than normal operations. Replacement factors and consumption rates must be addressed in the planning phase. Attention to the mix of class II and IV supplies, especially those used for decontamination and protection of personnel and logistic installations, is necessary. To anticipate requirements and forestall shortages, logistic officers must consider experience factors, known effects of NBC weapons, and enemy NBC capability.

Precise and detailed planning must provide for initial, on-hand requirements and a gradual buildup of supplies to fulfill later requirements. Buildup depends on the size of the force, size of the area available for logistic installations, tactical situation, and future plans. Initially, assault unit supplies are limited to a two- to three-day level.

Provisions also must be made to fill emergency requirements resulting from NBC attack. This is accomplished by providing a readily available supply reserve and arranging for emergency air delivery of supplies from rear area supply installations.

Water

Operating in protective clothing increases individual water consumption. Large amounts of nonpotable water are also needed for decontamination procedures. The availability of nonpotable water and nonaqueous decontaminates greatly improves the speed and efficiency of decontamination operations. Collocating NBC decontamination stations next to adequate sources of water should be a major planning consideration.

NBC Equipment

Intense planning must be given to supplying and maintaining NBC protection equipment (class II and class IV). The equipment addressed in the following subparagraphs requires special resupply considerations.

Chemical Protective Ensemble

The continued serviceability of contaminated chemical protective ensembles after chemical attack is limited. MOPP exchange or removal of the overgarment in a clean environment is required. It is best if MOPP exchange takes place as soon as possible after contamination. Disposal of contaminated protective ensembles must be planned for.

Mask Filters

In the field, the protective mask's combat filters are changed immediately after a blood agent attack, every 30 days, or as directed in an active NBC environment. Once removed from its sealed protective container, combat filters are replaced as indicated in table 3-1.

Table 3-1: Combat Filters Replacement Schedule

CLIMATE	ENVIRONMENT	TIMESPAN
Tropic	nonchemical	2 months
Temperate	nonchemical	12 months
Arctic	nonchemical	24 months

Decontamination Kits

A large supply of decontamination kits must be readily available. Decontamination kits are limited in their decontamination capability. One kit can decontaminate a small area or a few small items of personal equipment but can only provide partial decontamination of an individual.

Chemical Protective Gloves

Individuals are issued two pairs of chemical protective gloves for each set of chemical overgarments. Replace contaminated gloves when exchanging overgarments.

Chemical Protective Boots

Individuals are issued one pair of chemical protective boots for each set of chemical overgarments.

Resupply Request

The resupply request for protective overgarments should include requests for protective gloves and protective boots. Replace the boots when exchanging overgarments.

Maintenance

Units must be able to continue performing organizational maintenance of organic equipment in an NBC environment. The maintenance turnaround time may increase after an NBC attack because equipment must be decontaminated **before** performing maintenance.

Transportation

Planning must address maximum effective use of transportation. Some types of movement of units and equipment can provide the enemy with a concentrated target that is easily detected. Careful movement planning and execution can reduce the MAGTF's vulnerability to attack at such times. Planners should consider—

• Movement over multiple routes or by echelon to decrease concentration of forces.

- Assembly and movement under cover of darkness or during periods of reduced visibility.

- Use of covered and concealed routes.

- Speed of execution, particularly during loading and unloading.

- Use of smoke to screen assembly operations and movement.

- Scheduling movement to maintain unit separation.

- Controlling transport and support units engaged in NBC warfare (availability of sufficient and suitable vehicles, trailers, and aircraft).

- Equipment contamination increases transportation requirements.

- Mass casualty evacuations increase needs for motor transport assets.

- Overhead covers for vehicle operators provide additional protection.

- Training operators to avoid unnecessary concentrations of vehicles and to perform decontamination operations. This lessens their exposure to threat agents.

- Rerouting traffic to avoid contamination.

- Reducing the ratio between the amount of supplies delivered and the miles traveled by transportation units (reducing the need for decontamination).

- Multiple petroleum, oil, and lubricant transportation and storage facilities (e.g., port discharge facilities, tank farms) as a source of alternate transportation and backup facilities in the event of a chemical or biological strike.

- Plans to recover equipment from contaminated areas (include in operation plans and orders). This provides backup equipment for the front line if needed.

General Engineering

Protective measures prior to and damage resulting from NBC attack require additional engineering efforts. Reinforcement of division engineers by force engineer units is essential to effect successful engineer operations in forward areas. Engineer personnel and equipment are used to augment the formation of the provisional NBC platoon. Engineer personnel also assist in preparing thorough decontamination sites and participate in decontamination operations.

Health Service Support

NBC warfare has the potential to generate enormous workloads for the health service support (HSS) system. The most obvious impact is the increased number of patients treated and/or evacuated. HSS personnel, who are located with combat forces, will have to function in a NBC-contaminated environment. This will degrade an HSS unit's operational ability. To accomplish its mission, HSS personnel must carefully balance the following factors:

- The need to maintain maximum simplicity.
- Protection of patients and staff from unnecessary exposure to NBC agents.
- Decontamination of incoming patients.
- Rapid sorting of incoming patients.
- Unit mobility.
- Control of contamination within the facility.

Basic operational principles and procedures exist for all HSS facilities operating in a NBC warfare environment. Higher echelons of HSS are typically located in uncontaminated areas. HSS facilities are located with combat forces. It may be necessary for each individual HSS facility to modify its basic procedures based on the level and type of NBC threat in its operating environment. Supported units may augment HSS aid stations and other supporting HSS facilities with additional nonmedical personnel to sustain operations in a NBC-contaminated environment.

Since NBC warfare places large demands on the medical supply system and HSS personnel, management of chemical casualties ashore, afloat, and in transit requires a considerable manpower commitment. This commitment is never solely an HSS function. Supporting units establish and operate patient decontamination facilities. While these nonmedical personnel don't need medical training, they must be designated, trained, and rehearsed in their augmentation role. Without this additional manpower to assist in the decontamination of patients, medical facilities organic to Fleet Marine Force units are greatly restricted in the number of patients they can treat and in the treatment they can render.

NBC Injury Assessment

NBC attacks produce high casualty concentrations over a short period of time. Depending on the NBC agent's range and rate of action and the successful collection of casualties, NBC treatment facilities can receive large surges of NBC casualties. Treatment and evacuation of contaminated personnel are also complicated by limited evacuation capabilities and the allotment of available air frames and shipboard space for NBC casualties.

Once an NBC patient is received at the treatment facility, the patient's evaluation and treatment is complicated by the NBC protective equipment worn by both the patient and the treatment personnel. In addition to NBC exposure, a patient may suffer from traumatic injuries or other illnesses. The patient's NBC exposure must be treated without aggravating his other injuries or illnesses. Frequently, a clinical judgment must be made regarding which injury, wound, illness, or NBC exposure receives priority for treatment and/or evacuation. Lifesaving measures must be given priority over decontamination, despite the possibility of increased NBC injury caused by delay in specific treatment. Procedures to control hemorrhage, shock, respiratory, or other clinical conditions may equal or surpass the urgency to treat the NBC exposure. The recommended order of treatment priority is to—

- Restore/assist respiration.
- Control hemorrhage.
- Administer the appropriate antidote.
- Remove contaminated clothing as soon as possible.
- Decontaminate where required and as conditions permit.
- Protect from the elements as required.
- Treat shock, wounds, and illnesses that may endanger life if treatment is delayed.
- Evacuate patient as soon as possible.

Note
Blister agent casualties who have traumatic injuries or other illnesses should be decontaminated as early as possible.

Patient Decontamination

The most time-consuming task is decontamination of NBC casualties. This must be accomplished before medical treatment can be started. Decontamination techniques are contained in FMFM 11-10 and FMFM 11-11. Decontamination is necessary to prevent the spread of contamination and to protect personnel who come in contact with chemical casualties.

Decontamination is normally accomplished in the following sequence: self-aid, buddy aid, corpsman aid, aid station, and medical unit decontamination facility. Limited health care is provided to a contaminated patient prior to decontamination because of the danger that exists to both the patient and the HSS provider. Field trials, using simulated agents, have shown that attempts to perform even the most basic life sustaining procedures for a contaminated casualty are likely to cause additional NBC exposure to the patient and may expose the HSS provider to NBC agents. Procedures carried out before patient decontamination, or in the presence of a continuing NBC hazard, must be carefully weighed with due consideration to both the patient's and HSS personnel's welfare. However, casualties are never denied access to medical treatment or transportation based on their contamination level.

Medical Attention

During the ship-to-shore phase of an amphibious assault, medical care ashore is limited to a combat unit's organic medical sections. Medical care for the assault force is provided by corpsmen who land with the ground units. Since only a few medical personnel are ashore at this time, initial treatment by self-aid and buddy aid is an extremely important element of care. Casualties can be evacuated from the point of wounding/injury to a battalion aid station (BAS) or evacuation station, or they can be evacuated directly to a casualty receiving and treatment ship (CRTS). Since decontamination operations are extremely difficult during this period, all casualties coming from an area where chemical weapons have been employed are considered contaminated.

At the BAS, casualties are triaged and stabilized. HSS personnel usually work in full protective gear. Decontamination is attempted at an evacuation station only if facilities, manpower, and time are available. Triage is performed prior to decontamination to conserve medical manpower and to ensure that casualties are properly categorized and prioritized for further evacuation.

After establishment of a collecting and clearing company or surgical support company ashore, casualties evacuated from a BAS will flow through the medical battalion treatment facility. This is the first potential location for a casualty decontamination facility. Casualty decontamination sites must involve elements of the entire CSS organization, not just HSS elements. To function effectively, medical battalion treatment facilities must have collective protection shelters where medical care can be delivered to decontaminated casualties in an uncontaminated environment. Casualty decontamination facilities are staffed by personnel from the supported unit.

Trained NBC personnel supervise casualty decontamination facilities to ensure compliance with all decontamination regulations. Decontaminated casualties who have been stabilized and triaged are evacuated to a CRTS or to other rear areas for further treatment and disposition. If an airfield capable of handling fixed-wing transport aircraft is available, casualties may be evacuated out of the objective area. NBC protection may be required for casualties being evacuated.

Patient Evacuation

The evacuation of NBC-contaminated casualties presents a hazard to unprotected personnel. Personnel must wear their individual protective equipment while decontaminating or handling casualties. The general rule is, if you don't know their status, treat them as if they are contaminated.

Hospital corpsmen in an NBC environment endeavor to render appropriate emergency medical care to the wounded. They should attempt to determine if an agent antidote has been administered, the number of doses, and whether or not more is needed. The total number of doses given must be entered on the Field Medical Card (DD Form 1380). A corpsman must also attempt to determine if a casualty is contaminated and, if so, provide decontamination if possible. A corpsman seldom has the time or resources to accomplish significant decontamination.

Note
Corpsmen in the field must use DD Form 1380 to record all treatment and decontamination procedures.

Evacuation from Contaminated Areas

Air evacuation of contaminated casualties by helicopter is possible. Helicopters afford sufficient ventilation to prevent vapor buildup, but aircrews must use protective masks while transporting contaminated casualties. However, aircraft used to transport contaminated casualties must be decontaminated before transporting uncontaminated personnel. For that reason, air evacuation may be impractical in a tactical scenario where air assets are limited. If terrain permits, HSS personnel use ground transportation to evacuate contaminated casualties to aid stations and CSSE medical facilities.

Even if an aid station was not in the target area of an NBC attack, the station is considered to be operating in a contaminated environment whenever contaminated casualties or personnel have been present. An aid station quickly becomes a contaminated area because of the foot and vehicular traffic that transports casualties into the station. All equipment exposed to contamination is assumed contaminated and handled accordingly. Patients and HSS personnel must be protected from contact with contaminated equipment and personnel. FMFM 11-11 addresses protecting patients and HSS personnel from contamination. Patient protective wrap can function either as protection for the patient or protection from a contaminated patient. Care must be exercised, however, since any restriction in ventilation over a contaminated surface increases the degree of penetration of an agent into the surface (particularly human skin).

Evacuation from Contaminated to Uncontaminated Areas

HSS facilities above BAS level should be located in uncontaminated areas with access to higher levels of medical support. If an uncontaminated area cannot be found, a collecting and clearing company can function in a contaminated environment at reduced effectiveness if collective protection shelters are available and utilized. Even when operating in uncontaminated areas, both the collecting and clearing company and the surgical company must be organized and prepared to receive contaminated casualties.

Ambulances used to evacuate patients from supported units in a contaminated area must be considered contaminated. No contaminated vehicle should be allowed into the clean area without decontamination nor should a clean vehicle be allowed into a contaminated area unless it can be decontaminated before it exits the area. To ensure that other vehicles do not contaminate clean routes, selection of clean routes must be coordinated with regimental and division headquarters and the procedure included in unit SOPs. MAGTF operations by forward-deployed Marine expeditionary units (MEUs) may require that contaminated casualties be evacuated to the CRTS without thorough decontamination. This contingency requires close cooperation among the "blue-green" team and is addressed in MAGTF and damage control SOPs.

Biological Agent Concerns

Medical care for victims of toxin poisoning is limited and consists primarily of supportive care (i.e., preventing or treating shock). Cardiac and respiratory functions must be monitored and supported as necessary. Definitive medical care requires precise identification of the toxin, a capability not currently available in the field for all potential toxins. Antitoxin therapy is available for some toxins, but these are highly specific and cannot be administered until the toxin is identified. Until the toxin is identified, the patient must be given supportive treatment based on medical symptoms. Recovery times vary. For some toxins, prolonged recuperation periods are required. For other toxins, their effective periods are of a short duration and the victim may return to duty within hours.

Chapter 4

Passive and Active NBC Planning Measures

"In forming the plan of a campaign, it is requisite to fore-see everything the enemy may do, and be prepared with the necessary means to counteract it."[1]

—Napoleon

The introduction of NBC weapons into the modern battlespace has an impact on critical tactical considerations. An effective NBC vulnerability assessment assists the commander in the planning for and execution of appropriate active and passive NBC defensive measures in order to minimize adverse affects on the mission.

One important planning factor that affects both passive and active NBC planning is time. Combat support and CSS operations are more difficult to perform in an NBC environment. Tasks and missions take longer and require extensive training in MOPP gear; for example—

- A typical movement to contact could be hampered by contamination lying directly to the front of friendly forces.

- An amphibious force could be forced to conduct a tactical recovery of aircraft and personnel (TRAP) wearing MOPP IV gear.

- A combat resupply could be delayed for hours, or even days, because troops in the rear are performing decontamination operations of the logistic base.

Therefore, commanders must accurately estimate the time it takes to accomplish tasks/missions in an NBC environment. FMFM 11-9 provides tables that estimate the time it takes to accomplish tasks/missions in an NBC environment.

Other factors that affect planning include the physical changes to the battlespace because of NBC weapons. These obstacles can be overcome or dealt with through an effective intelligence preparation of the battle space (IPB). The IPB process provides the commander the situational awareness to plan ahead and employ appropriate NBC defense (passive and active) measures. MCRP 3-37.1A, *NBC Vulnerability Analysis*, provides details on the NBC IPB process. Units should have the following NBC analysis capabilities:

- Coordinate, maintain, and interpret NBC survey and radiological monitoring operations.

- Maintain NBC survey and radiological monitoring situation maps.

- Determine the immediate and cumulative NBC and radiological effects on personnel. This determination is based on NBC survey and radiological monitoring data.

- Disseminate radiological fallout and NBC information according to established intelligence handling procedures.

- Familiarize personnel with enemy NBC capabilities, organizations, weapons, equipment, techniques, and activities that could be indicative of an enemy's preparation for NBC attacks.

- Determine the effect of terrain and weather on enemy NBC capabilities and friendly employment of nuclear weapons on areas or routes intended for friendly troops.

- Investigate NBC attacks and furnish necessary reports.

During amphibious operations, the commander, amphibious task force, plans the overall NBC defensive measures for the amphibious task force. The commander, landing force, determines and prescribes active and passive NBC defensive measures to be used by the landing force. The commander, landing force, then presents to the commander, amphibious task force, the active defense measures that must be provided by other forces.

Passive Measures

To perform passive NBC actions, units down to the battalion/group level (unless otherwise directed) should have—

- An SOP for NBC defensive operations.
- Collective defense measures. This includes proper NBC discipline; protection of food, water, and equipment; and proper use of sentinels near shelters, sleeping personnel, working parties, and convoys.
- Qualified personnel to teach and supervise the use of NBC protective equipment.
- Personnel familiar with the effects of friendly nuclear weapons and duration of effects.
- Methods of dealing with (avoidance and decontamination) NBC-contaminated areas and equipment.
- The ability to make command decisions for filter replacement based on average exposure of unit personnel.
- The ability, at battalion/group level and higher, to recommend the allowable radiation dosage for an operation.

Passive NBC action are discussed in the following subparagraphs.

Avoid Detection

Troops must use effective operations security measures (e.g., camouflage, cover and concealment, light discipline, signal security) to avoid becoming a target for NBC weapons.

Avoid Contamination

Contamination avoidance is the action taken to detect and identify contamination hazards. It provides the MAGTF commander with an early warning capability that allows the MAGTF commander to maneuver forces and avoid contamination. It is one of the most important aspects of NBC defense.

Units must be able to locate clear areas and rapidly identify contaminated ones. Reconnaissance units detect and identify hazards forward of the front line of troops. Timely detection and warning, detailed monitoring, and surveying (NBC reconnaissance) allow a commander to bypass obstacles that could delay and potentially defeat the force. This also reduces time and effort in exercising decontamination procedures.

NBC attacks can create high casualties, material losses, and obstacles to movement in the battlespace. NBC defense training that focuses on contamination avoidance can reduce many of these problems. FMFM 11-18 and FM 3-19/FMFM 11-20, *NBC Reconnaissance*, provide detailed information on contamination avoidance.

Provide Early Warning and Accurate Reporting

Early warning of an NBC attack, or advanced warning of the arrival of an NBC hazard, is essential to mission accomplishment. Once an NBC hazard is identified, rapid dissemination to other units is vital.

Instill Confidence

A Marine's confidence in the ability to function in an NBC environment greatly increases chances of survival. Training must be conducted in various levels of MOPP to achieve this confidence. A Marine must be physically and mentally conditioned to overcome the shock of NBC warfare.

Seek Protection

Natural terrain can provide shelter from the effects of NBC weapons. Ditches, ravines, and natural depressions reduce initial nuclear effects, but chemical agents tend to accumulate in these areas. Heavy forests and jungles protect against liquid chemical agents, but increase the effectiveness of vapor agents. Fighting holes with overhead cover and shelters offer the best protection against NBC weapons. Any overhead cover such as tents, tarpaulins, and ponchos offer at least some protection from fallout and liquid chemical agents. Collective protective shelters and those vehicles equipped with collective protective systems offer the best protection.

Disperse Troops

CSS installations and troops in compact assembly areas are extremely vulnerable to NBC weapons. Commanders must determine a balance between dispersion to reduce vulnerability and the operational necessity to concentrate troop location.

Remain Mobile

Constant movement prevents the enemy from pinpointing locations. Tactical mobility gives the commander the best chance for avoidance.

Cover Supplies and Equipment

Store supplies and equipment under cover to avoid contamination. Buildings offer excellent protection. Field expedient methods of covering supplies and equipment can include canvas tarps, plastic covers, ponchos, water bladder covers, and drop cloths.

Limit Exposure

The amount of exposure in a NBC operation is critical. All plans should include post-attack procedures that limit exposure to NBC hazards. Every minute spent in a radiologically-contaminated environment increases a person's total radiation dosage. The longer a person is exposed to NBC contamination, the greater the chances of becoming a casualty.

Update Immunizations

Immunizations reduce the chance of a Marine becoming a biological casualty. Proper immunizations protect against most known, disease-producing biological agents. All Marines receive basic immunizations during recruit training, and their health records reflect the immunizations received. Medical personnel should periodically screen individual health records and keep them up to date. If Marines are deploying to areas in which specific diseases are prevalent, additional immunization may need to be obtained.

Provide Individual Protection

Each individual Marine must be properly equipped with individual protective clothing and equipment and be proficient in its use. The minimum requirements are—

- Protective mask (appropriate mask for the mission) and appropriate accessories.
- Protective ensemble (suit, gloves, and footwear covers).
- Protective hood and/or second skin.
- Individual decontamination kit.
- Individual antidotes against chemical agent poisoning.
- Individual dosimeter (one per four Marines).

Provide Collective Protection

Collective protection is the use of shelters to provide a contamination-free environment for selected portions of the force. Collective protection should be an integral part of NBC countermeasures. It provides a contamination-free working environment and allows relief from the continuous wearing of protective clothing. See FMFM 11-9.

Active Measures

Aggressive, timely, and complete destruction of enemy NBC employment-capable forces remains the single most effective NBC defensive measure. Generally, active protective measures employed against conventional enemy attack are implemented into the NBC defense plan to—

- Destroy enemy launching sites.
- Increase air defense measures.
- Increase air and ground reconnaissance.

The following active measures enhance a unit's ability to operate in tactical operations with an increased level of confidence while in an NBC environment.

Detection

NBC detection is part of conventional reconnaissance. In addition to looking for enemy activity, reconnaissance elements also check for contamination. Unit reconnaissance efforts can detect and locate most NBC hazards if all reconnaissance teams include a detection capability. Marines down to the battalion/selected squadron level operate NBC detection equipment as an additional duty. At the company/squadron level, they organize into teams of two or three Marines. These teams provide local commanders with NBC detection information (i.e., where contaminated areas might be or where clean areas are located). Data collected by these teams is forwarded to higher headquarters. These teams also identify or mark contaminated areas for follow-on troops. If contamination exists, the commander must evaluate the type and degree of NBC hazard and how it could affect operations.

Detection means may vary. Current capabilities allow the MAGTF to employ both point (radiological and chemical) and standoff (chemical) detectors. Proper training and employment of point and standoff detectors, intelligence information, and weather conditions aid in the detection of NBC hazards. Point detectors indicate that contamination exists at a point where the operator employs the detector. Standoff detectors alert commanders that contamination may be present at some distance, up to 5 kilometers, from where the detector is employed. A standoff detector provides the commander with additional time to maneuver the force or to place them into the appropriate protective posture.

There are three reconnaissance methods used during NBC detection:

- Route reconnaissance provides detailed information of all terrain surrounding a given route. The enemy's attack on this route could restrict movement of friendly forces. With accurate and timely contamination plots of a route, commanders can avoid contamination or direct a reduction in MOPP.

- Area reconnaissance provides missing NBC information on a specific area. The area location and required information must be specified.

- Zone reconnaissance is performed if little information is available concerning enemy dispositions across a wide area. It can provide detailed information concerning all routes, obstacles, terrain, and enemy forces. The commander's concept for maneuver and fire support may be influenced if known NBC obstacles are astride a prospective axis of advance.

Decontamination

Decontamination is required when contamination avoidance is not successful or is not an option. Decontamination operations are conducted to decontaminate individuals and/or equipment.

These operations are time-consuming and logistic intensive. Commanders must balance the needs of the tactical situation against available decontamination options when planning the employment of the force.

To reduce the spread of contamination, commanders limit the number of personnel and equipment allowed in an area and try to confine the contaminated area to as small an area as possible. This reduces the amount of decontamination required. The following subparagraphs identify the three categories of decontamination operations.

Immediate Decontamination (Basic Marine Skills)

Successful decontamination operations begin with the basic skills that ensure individual survival. Basic Marine skills include skin decontamination, personal wipe down, and operator's spray down. These skills instill confidence in the individual Marine, and this confidence allows a Marine to function and survive in an NBC environment.

Operational Decontamination

Operational decontamination includes vehicle wash down and MOPP gear exchange. It is performed by organic units drawn from the organization that requires decontamination. Operational decontamination can allow a force to continue to fight even after it receives multiple exposures to contamination.

Thorough Decontamination

Thorough decontamination is conducted when operational decontamination will not suffice. Thorough decontamination includes detailed troop decontamination and detailed equipment decontamination. Combining operational decontamination procedures (MOPP exchange) and thorough decontamination (detailed equipment decontamination) may provide the MAGTF commander with a more supportable NBC plan.

Sustained combat operations in an NBC environment are possible only if commanders understand the levels of decontamination operations. Decontamination is successful only when appropriate command and support relationships are understood by NBC specialists, shower unit/hygienists, and appropriate equipment operators. FMFM 11-10 provides detailed decontamination procedures.

If a subordinate unit requests reinforcement to perform decontamination operations, the division provisional decontamination unit provides additional personnel to the requesting unit. This consists of, but is not limited to, a nucleus from the division NBC platoon and augmentation by shower/hygiene specialists and their equipment from the combat engineer battalion. Similar support for the remainder of the MAGTF, such as additional reinforcement of the ACE or GCE and thorough decontamination, are provided by the CSSE provisional decontamination unit. This unit is created from the nucleus of the CSSE NBC platoon and augmented by shower/hygiene specialists. Their equipment is from the engineer support battalion.

Other Service Support

As situations escalate and the requirement to introduce follow-on forces into theater increases, the need for airfields, ports, and other facilities also increases. As an expeditionary force, the Marine Corps concentrates its efforts toward operational decontamination. Thorough decontamination of airfields, ports, and facilities is a joint effort. Host nation support, along with elements of other Services, provides the bulk of the manpower and equipment required for thorough decontamination of fixed facilities. Marine Corps forces provide assistance as required.

Chapter 5

NBC Defense Training

"In no other profession are the penalties for employing untrained personnel so appal[l]ing or so irrevocable as in the military."[1]

—Douglas MacArthur

The Marine Corps trains its personnel to accomplish their wartime mission in any battlespace condition. Anytime we separate NBC from other training events, we condition Marines to regard NBC defense operations as a separate form of warfare. The Marine Corps does not conduct NBC warfare; it conducts warfare in an NBC environment. NBC readiness is a command responsibility; therefore, concentrated training, drills, and exercises must be integrated into wargaming scenarios and individual unit training to ensure a thorough understanding of NBC defense operations and procedures. Every Marine must be trained to recognize NBC attacks, mask and don protective clothing quickly, perform assigned missions wearing protective clothing, and survive for extended periods in an NBC environment. All Marine Corps organizations must continually integrate NBC defense training to develop unit integrity, cohesion, and NBC defense operational expertise.

Objectives

NBC training starts at the entry level. At recruit training and The Basic School, Marines are introduced to the field protective mask and the gas chamber. NBC training is a command responsibility. Commanders must ensure that every Marine receives thorough, well-integrated NBC training in order to protect himself, fellow Marines, and equipment. Adding an NBC specialist to a unit will not ensure the safety of an entire unit during an NBC attack or increase a unit's NBC standards or proficiency level. The only way to achieve NBC proficiency and maintain NBC standards is to conduct a comprehensive training program that addresses the individual Marine. To be successful, this program must be actively supported by the unit commander. Both individual and unit training must be conducted. Training objectives must enable an individual/unit to—

- Determine, identify, warn, and take proper defensive actions against NBC hazards and attacks as prescribed in unit SOPs.

- Avoid, cross, or function in contaminated areas with minimum risk and decontaminate as necessary.

- Withstand enemy NBC attack with minimum interference to the assigned mission.

- Perform the assigned mission(s) while the unit is in various levels of MOPP.

- Decontaminate personnel and equipment.

- Use the NBC hazard prediction system to predict downwind hazards resulting from an NBC-related attack.

- Apply proper protection procedures before, during, and after an enemy NBC attack.

- Submit NBC 1, NBC 3, and NBC 4 reports promptly and properly.

- Maintain NBC protection, detection, and decontamination equipment.

Training Considerations

The conduct of unit NBC defense training varies due to local conditions. However, certain basic training methods hold true regardless of the type of unit or its location.

Focus on Fundamentals

Instruction in NBC defense should concentrate on the fundamental skills needed to survive and continue the mission in an NBC environment.

Apply Sound Training Principles

Effective NBC training is realized only if the fundamentals of good military instruction are followed. What is taught in the classroom should be used in practice exercises and in actual missions. Classroom instruction should make maximum use of actual NBC equipment as training aids and provide Marines with the knowledge needed to conduct training in the field.

Incorporate Practical Exercises

Although it is possible to learn the basics of NBC defense operations through lectures, films, and demonstrations, the best learning tool is practical exercise. Each Marine must be provided with as many firsthand experiences as possible. Marines should perform actual protective measures, not merely be exposed to procedural information. For example, have each Marine demonstrate how to use a field protective mask.

Use Ingenuity

Due to variations in local conditions, an individual Marine's background, and unit's mission, a set series of problems or training aides will not satisfactorily fulfill all training requirements. Meaningful training situations require the application of imagination and initiative by all concerned. Existing manuals and other training literature can provide training situations that can be used for NBC defense training.

Strive for Realism

Training exercises should resemble, as closely as possible, the expected combat conditions during the mission. For example, during combat, an NBC attack usually occurs without warning and in conjunction with other attacks. An effective training exercise prepares Marines to react properly to a surprise NBC attack.

Use Munitions and Simulants Properly

Proper use of munitions and simulants can be an effective training tool that instills the individual Marine with confidence in NBC defense equipment and skills. Improper use of training munitions and simulants hamper NBC defense training and makes it harder to schedule and provide training in the future.

Use Concurrent Training

Concurrent training is the simultaneous training of part of a unit in one or more subjects in addition to the primary subject. It is an efficient use of time and training opportunities. Concurrent training allows the G-3/S-3 and the NBC officer to increase the number of NBC defense training hours without extending unit training schedules. Training periods can occur during scheduled or unplanned delays in an exercise or training schedule; therefore, the NBC section should always be ready to take advantage of unexpected opportunities with appropriate "hippocket" instruction to maximize training and NBC readiness. Although not related directly to the primary training mission, concurrent training should always meet other individual/unit training objectives. Concurrent NBC training is used to—

- Emphasize that an NBC environment is only one characteristic of the overall battlespace.

- Emphasize that NBC operations are not a stand-alone form of warfare; they must be included in all types of training whenever possible.

- Instill confidence. The individual Marine must have confidence in the assigned protective equipment and the ability to successfully survive an NBC attack, but the individual Marine must also respect NBC agents.

- Complete and maintain qualifications prescribed by standards of proficiency (Marine Corps Combat Readiness Evaluation System standards).

- Ensure Marines develop and maintain individual and unit capabilities.

Integrate Field Exercises and Maneuvers

The integration of NBC defense scenarios into field exercises and maneuvers gives Marines an opportunity to apply their classroom training and to develop confidence in their ability to accomplish the mission in the presence of NBC hazards. Commanders should ensure that the following criteria have been met before field exercises and maneuvers involving NBC defense situations are executed:

- Marines are proficient in NBC defense measures.

- NBC defense situations are introduced after the fundamentals of the primary subject area have been mastered and an initial proficiency has been attained.

- NBC defense situations are integrated so that they provide personnel with the ability to achieve the training objectives in the particular subject area under NBC conditions.

- The NBC situation is tactically sound, and integrated problems are simple and realistic. (The NBC defense situation should be one that a Marine could expect to encounter in an actual combat situation.)

- Possible effects of the NBC defense situation on the primary training program have been defined.

While preparing an integrated NBC exercise and organizing support material, the G-3/S-3/NBC officer must—

- Select the principal subject of training and appropriate NBC defense subject(s) for integration.

- State the degree or status of training that personnel have had in the principal subject and the selected NBC defense subject.

- Create a situation that could exist in combat.

- Determine objectives for the scheduled training.

- Describe the integration action performed.

- List actions expected of personnel.

Commanders should ensure that the NBC defense situation and primary training issues are critiqued when the exercise is concluded.

Training Requirements

Individual and unit team training is essential to attain the proficiency required to survive and win in an NBC environment. To ensure that individuals and units are prepared for NBC defense, commands must conduct periodic inspections. See MCO 3400.3, *Nuclear, Biological, and Chemical (NBC) Defense Training*, for details and checklists. Inspections are field-oriented and tailored to determine a unit's overall readiness capability.

NBC Control Center Elements

NBC control center elements within the division, wing, FSSG, MAGTF, and subordinate units conduct training based on operations and duties specified in chapter 2. Training of NBC control center personnel includes instruction in NBC control center operations, basic fallout prediction, operational aspects of residual nuclear effects, and prediction and plotting of downwind toxic hazards. Training exercises monitor control center teams as they function in realistic operational situations. Control center teams' responses and decisions are reviewed and, if necessary, corrected.

NBC Monitor/Survey Team

Monitor/survey units detect and identify hazards forward of the front line of troops. They provide the MAGTF commander with an early warning capability that allows maneuvering of the force and avoids contamination. Training that simulates potential operational conditions ensures that teams are qualified to handle and operate current radiac equipment, chemical agent detector kits and devices, and biological sampling kits. A thorough knowledge of personnel monitoring, conduct of surveys, agent characteristics, and first aid procedures is mandatory. Monitor/survey team training focuses on the methods and procedures needed to avoid contaminated areas, which reduces the force's decontamination requirements.

Decontamination Team

Decontamination team training focuses on the proper donning of protective suits, decontamination drills that involve table of equipment reagents, proper removal of chemical protective suits, and personnel decontamination procedures.

NBC Platoons/Sections (Provisional NBC Companies)

NBC platoon elements are required to conduct quarterly NBC drills. To enhance the instructional value of the drills, unit NBC officers plan and rehearse defensive operations with key staff members/small unit leaders. This training includes a practice NBC alert warning, issue/simulated issue of individual protective NBC equipment, formation and assembly of NBC teams, and assembly of unit personnel in preassigned or hasty shelter areas.

Annual drills should be scheduled that involve all components of the MAGTF. These drills should draw personnel and equipment assets from within the MAGTF to form provisional NBC defense units. These units can be placed in either a general or direct support role.

NBC Equipment Surveillance Unit

The nuclear, biological, and chemical equipment surveillance unit (NBC ESU) provides physical testing of selected NBC defense equipment. It also provides instruction/consultation on how to use NBC defense equipment serviceability standards to all Marine Corps activities. See MCO 3960.5, *Nuclear, Biological, and Chemical (NBC) Defense Equipment Test and Evaluation Program*, for information on the mission and support provided by the NBC ESU. Technical Instruction (T/I) 10010-20/5, *Serviceability Standards: Nuclear, Biological, and Chemical Defense Property*, provides information on serviceability standards for NBC-related equipment.

Appendix A

Sample Format of Appendix 2 to Annex C (Nuclear, Biological, and Chemical Defense Operations)

CLASSIFICATION

Copy no. _____ of _____ copies
Issuing headquarters
PLACE OF ISSUE
Date/time group
Message reference number

APPENDIX 2 (NBC Defense) to ANNEX C (Operations) to _____ Operations Order (U)

Ref: List standing instructions regarding defense against nuclear, biological, and chemical (NBC) weapons.

Time Zone:

1. Situation
   This paragraph consists of a description of the general NBC situation and sets the stage for the operation. It is always divided into three subparagraphs: enemy forces; missions and locations of higher, adjacent, and supporting friendly forces; and attachments and detachments. A fourth subparagraph that lists assumptions is included if an operation plan is used.

(Page number)
CLASSIFICATION

CLASSIFICATION

a. Enemy Forces

    (1) Annex B (Intelligence).

    (2) Current intelligence summaries.

    (3) Capabilities. Summarize the enemy's order of battle, and identify any area the enemy may subject to NBC attack. Estimate the enemy's ability to produce and employ NBC weapons. Identify the enemy's available delivery means, munitions stocks, and defensive equipment. Also, identify the enemy's ability to provide defensive support (e.g., decontamination of his combat support units).

    (4) Courses of action. Identify any enemy, NBC-specific course of action that could interfere with the accomplishment of the mission or affect implementation of the operation plan.

b. Friendly Forces. Estimate the NBC defensive capability of allied forces, government agencies, and civilian populations that may affect mission accomplishment. If applicable, address participation of allied forces, particularly if they require support from U.S. forces. Identify location and mission of nonorganic higher, adjacent, and supporting friendly forces that could influence the operation.

c. Attachments and Detachments. Identify NBC units attached to, or organic units detached from, the issuing headquarters. This can include division and force service

CLASSIFICATION

support group (FSSG) NBC platoon elements attached in support of subordinate units, or Marine wing support squadron elements and who they support. This paragraph also addresses any attachments from outside the command (e.g., detachment from the FSSG NBC platoon in support of the ground combat element). See Annex A (Task Organization).

d. <u>Assumptions</u>. List the assumptions on which NBC defense planning is based (e.g., it takes longer to operate in an NBC environment).

2. <u>Mission</u>
Mission provided by higher command and its purpose. (State the mission to be accomplished by NBC defense in support of the overall mission.)

3. <u>Execution</u>
Indicate how the issuing command will accomplish its mission. Specifically, this paragraph provides a brief summary of the commander's overall concept of operations, assigns definite tactical missions to each of the command's tactical units or task groups, and includes coordination details.

a. <u>Concept of Operations</u>. Provide a general summary of how the commander intends to execute the operation. This paragraph outlines the scheme of maneuver, sequence of events, plan for employment of supporting arms, and landing plan (if amphibious or helicopter operations).

(Page number)
CLASSIFICATION

CLASSIFICATION

b. <u>Tasks</u>. Provide a listing of staff responsibilities. Staff responsibilities do not change in an NBC environment. In addition to the regular staff responsibilities, the following NBC-specific tasks must also be addressed:

(1) <u>G-1/S-1</u>

(a) Provide for handling of enemy prisoners of war (EPWs). Coordinate with the NBC defense officer to provide EPWs with chemical protective clothing.

(b) Coordinate priority of assignment for nuclear, biological, and chemical detachment (NBCD) personnel with the NBCD officer.

(2) <u>G-2/S-2</u>

(a) Effect the production and dissemination of intelligence in the following areas:

<u>1.</u> Enemy NBC weapons and delivery systems.

<u>2.</u> Enemy NBC equipment and training status.

<u>3.</u> Enemy intent to use NBC weapons.

<u>4.</u> Enemy ability to produce NBC weapons.

(b) Initiate activities to degrade and counter the enemy's ability to acquire friendly targets for NBC attack.

CLASSIFICATION

(3) <u>G-3/S-3</u>

    (a) Prepare operation plans/orders to implement the commander's guidance for NBCD operations.

    (b) Ensure NBCD standing operating procedures (SOPs) are reviewed and updated by assigned NBCD personnel.

    (c) Activate the NBCD control center and coordinate its activities with other sections.

    (d) Consider the NBC threat when determining the general location of the command post.

    (e) Coordinate the use of alarms with local governments to eliminate conflicting alarms.

    (f) Determine replacement priorities, including unit replacements, in coordination with G-1/S-1.

    (g) Coordinate the recommendation for a minimum, mission-oriented protective posture (MOPP) level with the NBC officer.

(4) <u>G-4/S-4</u>

    (a) Disperse logistic support facilities to reduce vulnerability to NBC weapons.

    (b) Plan for increased transportation requirements due to the dispersion of units, increased demand for NBCD equipment, and decontamination logistic requirements.

CLASSIFICATION

(c) Ensure availability of NBCD equipment.

(d) Supervise maintenance of NBCD equipment.

(e) Develop plans to transport increased numbers of casualties and contaminated casualties.

(f) Coordinate with higher headquarters for large-scale, thorough decontamination operations in response to an NBC attack.

(5) G-6/S-6. Ensure net utilization of NBC traffic is included in the communications-electronics annex.

(6) Medical Officer.

(a) Prescribe treatment procedures and ensure that facilities for treatment of NBC casualties are available.

(b) Make recommendations to prevent, and take actions to detect, contamination of food and water supplies.

(c) Direct the collecting and processing of biological samples for later identification.

(d) Oversee periodic monitoring of health records to ensure up-to-date immunizations of all personnel against potential biological agents. Verify that personnel requiring optical inserts have them.

CLASSIFICATION

    (e) Ensure training of medical personnel in the treatment of NBC casualties.

    (f) Coordinate, with the G-4/S-4, the procurement and distribution of medical supplies needed to treat NBC casualties.

    (g) Coordinate, with the G-4/S-4, to develop plans for the handling and movement of contaminated casualties.

    (h) Plan and supervise medical treatment for EPWs and civilian internees/detainees that may have been exposed to NBC agents.

    (i) Recommend when to begin taking nerve agent pyridostigmine pretreatment (NAPP) tablets.

c. <u>Major Subordinate Commander</u>. List the specific tasks assigned to each major subordinate commander. This paragraph should also list tasks of individual units as well as tasks of supporting establishments. At a minimum, this paragraph should address:

    (1) Decontamination capabilities.

    (2) Aerial survey capabilities.

    (3) NBC reconnaissance.

CLASSIFICATION

    (4) Augmentation.

    (5) Training.

d. <u>Reserve</u>. List all elements in the reserve unit and what they can contribute.

e. <u>Coordinating Instructions</u>. When two or more elements of the command are involved in the same NBC mission, coordinating instructions, which provide guidance and establish procedures applicable to NBC defense, are required. This paragraph provides tactical instruction and details of coordination; it also should address the following:

    (1) Location of primary and alternate decontamination sites.

    (2) Restrictions regarding the use of standard and non-standard decontaminants.

    (3) Essential elements of information.

    (4) Time attachments and/or detachments are effective.

    (5) Detection of NBC contamination.

    (6) Procedures for collecting NBC samples.

    (7) Method of collection.

CLASSIFICATION

(8) Chemical agent antidotes issued and issuing procedures established (e.g., when to administer: prior to, during, or after exposure).

(9) Inoculations administered, and by whom.

(10) Reports required by the issuing headquarters.

(11) Unit and individual NBC equipment required to accomplish the mission.

(12) Establishment of MOPP levels.

(13) Establishment of protection facilities and locations.

(14) Local alarms and warning procedures used by civilians.

4. Administration and Logistics

a. Supply. List supply procedures and responsibilities for NBC defense equipment. Address intratheater receipt, prepositioning, requisitioning, issue, accountability, and denial or evacuation procedures.

b. Storage and Transportation. List storage and transportation procedures, locations, and responsibilities for NBC defense equipment. This paragraph can address what gear is carried by the individual Marine and what equipment follows in the follow-on echelons.

(Page number)
CLASSIFICATION

CLASSIFICATION

c. Support for Allies and Friendly Forces. List procedures and responsibilities for providing NBC defensive logistic support to allied/friendly forces (if applicable). Address allied force familiarization or training (if necessary).

d. Medical Support. Based on the basic plan, outline procedures and responsibilities for providing medical support in the NBC environment. Refer to Annex Q for medical details.

5. Command and Signal
This paragraph provides instructions for the establishment and maintenance of communications and information concerning command installations and procedures. It also addresses command post locations and command post reporting, code words, recognition signals, identification plan, liaison procedures, and command relationships.

a. Command Relationships. Use this paragraph if the size or complexity of the operation dictates the use of unique command relationships. This paragraph also addresses the specific procedures used to obtain conditional release authority and approval for riot control agents and herbicide operations. If riot control agents and herbicides are used, identify the appropriate delegation of authority (for usage).

b. Signal. Refer the reader to Annex K for general signal requirements. Annex K can also contain special instructions relative to the use of radios, pyrotechnics, or other communication means required for NBC defense.

(Page number)
CLASSIFICATION

CLASSIFICATION

c. <u>Command Echelons</u>

    (1) Give locations of command echelons of the issuing unit and the subordinate unit, when known.

    (2) Include the location of higher and adjacent unit command posts (control centers).

    (3) Direct units to report new decontamination sites when established or to report and identify primary and alternate decontamination sites as established.

       /s/_____

Tabs: (Note: Formats for the following tabs can be found in MCRP 3-37A, *NBC Field Handbook.*)
   A– Unit NBC Reporting Sequence
   B– NBC 1 Report Format
   C– NBC 2 Report Format
   D– NBC 3 Report Format
   E– NBC 4 Report Format
   F– NBC 5 Report Format
   G– NBC 6 Report Format
   H– Chemical Downwind Message Format

DISTRIBUTION:

(Page number)
CLASSIFICATION

(reverse blank)

Marine Corps Chemical/Biological Incident Response Force

In July 1995, the Commandant of the Marine Corps identified the need for a strategic organization that would respond to the growing chemical/biological terrorist threat. As a result, the Marine Corps Chemical/Biological Incident Response Force (CBIRF) was created. Although the CBIRF has an established T/O and T/E, its capabilities continue to evolve. The following information provides the MAGTF commander with an overview of the CBIRF concept of unit employment.

Mission

The CBIRF is a national asset, staffed by the Marine Corps, with the capability to rapidly deploy to chemical or biological incidents. It is designed to assist the on-scene commander by providing initial post-incident consequence management.

Organization

The CBIRF consists of approximately 372 Navy and Marine Corps personnel under a single commander. This self-contained response force has six elements:

- Command.
- Chemical and biological reconnaissance.
- Decontamination.
- Medical.
- Security.
- Service support.

A unique feature of the CBIRF is its electronic linkage to an advisory group of experts. The advisory group, composed of civilian chemical/biological and disaster response experts, advises the CBIRF during training and incident response. Additionally, the CBIRF is supported by a deployable laboratory from the Navy Medical Research Institute, which can detect and identify biological agents.

Concept of Employment

The CBIRF's concept of employment addresses initial, rapid response to chemical/biological incidents on a worldwide basis. CBIRF's preferred method of employment is to be pre-staged for events of national interest or as a result of a credible threat. When a chemical/biological incident occurs, the CBIRF deploys to the affected site by the most expeditious means available. Once at the incident site, the CBIRF will provide the following capabilities:

- Assistance to the on-scene command in coordination of initial relief efforts.
- Security and isolation at the affected site (dependent on the size of the site).
- Detection and identification of military/toxic industrial chemical agents, biological agents, and radiological materials.
- Expert medical advice and assistance to local medical authorities.
- Service support assistance as required.
- Personnel decontamination for force personnel and victims of a WMD incident.
- Limited equipment decontamination.
- Casualty search and extraction.

These capabilities are directly tied to the work/rest cycles and the availability of support from on-scene authorities. Throughout the response, the CBIRF will be advised electronically by the advisory group and can be readily augmented by other Marine Corps and Navy units as necessary.

When not participating in exercises or actually committed to an incident response, the CBIRF will provide training teams to Navy and Marine units and installations to improve the Department of the Navy's overall state of chemical/biological training.

(reverse blank)

NBC Physiological Effects

Nuclear Weapons and Their Effects

During a nuclear detonation, casualties and material damage are caused by the blast wave, thermal and nuclear radiation, and light. The degree of damage depends on the type of weapon, height of the burst, distance from detonation, hardness of the target, and explosive yield of the weapon.

Blast Wave

At a fraction of a second after a nuclear detonation, a high pressure wave develops and moves outward from the fireball. This blast wave causes most of the destruction that accompanies a nuclear burst.

Thermal Radiation

Within less than a millionth of a second after detonation of a nuclear weapon, hot weapon residues radiate great amounts of energy. This extreme heat causes severe skin burns at great distances from ground zero.

Nuclear Radiation

Initial nuclear radiation occurs within the first minute after detonation. The initial radiation wave travels considerable distances through the air and produces harmful effects in humans. These penetrating rays damage tissue and blood-forming cells. An individual may receive a lethal or incapacitating dose of initial radiation before initiating protective measures. Radiation that lasts after the first minute and consists primarily of fallout and neutron-induced radiation is classified as residual nuclear radiation. The primary source of residual radiation is from fallout. Refer to FMFM 11-18 for details of nuclear radiation.

Light

The fireball from a nuclear detonation produces an extremely bright light. This light can cause temporary or permanent blindness. Blindness resulting from a daylight burst will probably be of a short duration. Blindness occurring from a night burst lasts for a longer period because the pupils allow more light to enter the eyes at night. The light flash also can cause permanent burn injury within the eye or permanent blindness. Typically, this occurs if an individual is looking toward the fireball during detonation.

Biological Agents and Their Effects

Biological warfare is the intentional use of micro-organisms, or their toxic products to cause death, disease, disability, or damage to man, animals, plants, or material. The strategic objective of biological warfare agents is to reduce the fighting capability of combat forces. The objective is accomplished by killing or incapacitating troops, by creating food and supply shortages, and by killing or incapacitating logistics personnel.

The world's major military powers and several Third World countries can produce and employ biological agents on a massive scale. Their use can quickly overload medical treatment facilities. Traditionally, biological weapons required an incubation period to develop their full destructive power (i.e., the biological agent had to multiply in its host before illness could be seen in the target population). This is no longer the case. Today, biological agents include toxins that do not have incubation periods and genetic engineering allows harmless organisms to produce toxic compounds.

Types

Biological agents are classified as pathogens, toxins, or bioregulators/modulators (BRMs). Pathogens or toxins can be either lethal or incapacitating (see Classification). Because pathogens are live agents and toxins (even though of biological origin) are nonliving biochemical compounds, there are major differences in their toxicity, stability, lethality, time to affect, and persistence in the field.

Pathogens

Pathogens are disease-producing micro-organisms that can occur naturally (bacteria, mycoplasma, rickettsia, fungi, viruses), or they can be altered by genetic engineering.

Toxins

Toxins are organic chemicals produced by different types of living organisms that are highly poisonous to man. Toxins are stable, readily available, and easy to manage, which is extremely important in biological warfare.

Bioregulators/Modulators

BRMs are chemical compounds that occur naturally in organisms. These compounds cause normal body responses such as sleep, fear and anxiety. BRMs can be used in relatively small amounts with intense effects.

Classification

Biological agents are classified according to their biological type, use, operational effect, and physiological action. Persistent and nonpersistent are terms used to describe the continuing hazard posed by the agent remaining in the environment. See FMFM 11-11 for details on the characteristics of biological agents.

Lethal Agents

Lethal biological agents, if untreated, could be expected to produce a high number of deaths. Mortality rates vary according to a number of factors, such as characteristics of the agent, route of entry, dose received, and, in the case of pathogens, the ability of the host to resist infection.

Incapacitating Agents

Incapacitating agents usually do not kill healthy adults, although death can occur in the very young or the infirm. Incapacitating agents can produce infection or disease with militarily significant disabilities among susceptible, exposed individuals.

Transmissible Agents

Some pathogens produce diseases that may be transmitted from person to person, which can lead to an epidemic. Other pathogens occur primarily in animals, but they can be transmitted to humans. Transmissible agents are important biological antipersonnel agents because the average person has very little natural/acquired immunity.

Operational Effects

The effects produced by biological agents can influence the continued operational effectiveness of units in the field. A healthy body's natural immunity can overcome small invasions of pathogenic organisms. However, without a specific, acquired immunity, the body cannot overcome a massive invasion of disease organisms released in a successful biological warfare attack.

Physiological Effects

Due to the incubation period of biological agents, the effects of disease-producing micro-organisms are delayed for varying periods of time after exposure. This delay is usually expressed as a range of time during which symptoms of a specific disease are expected to appear. Each biological warfare causative agent has an incubation period associated with the specific disease it is intended to produce. Massive doses of an agent may shorten an incubation period and alter the progress of the disease. The introduction of a disease-producing organism through a route of entry not natural for the specific disease may alter symptoms to such a degree that the disease may not be quickly recognized by a physician.

Places where micro-organisms enter the body are known as routes of entry. The three most important routes of entry are the skin, respiratory tract, and digestive tract. The body's respiratory system is the most susceptible to penetration because of the lungs' large surface area, the one-cell layer of alveolar sacs, and the tremendous blood supply. The body is better prepared to resist an invasion through the digestive tract and the skin. Penetration through the skin and mucous membranes may occur, particularly if the surface is abraded. Toxins also can invade the body through the skin and mucous membranes. The clinical effects of toxins can closely resemble those of chemical warfare agents. Toxins of military significance include neurotoxins or cytotoxins.

Neurotoxins

Neurotoxins interfere with nerve impulse transmissions and can be referred to as nerve toxins. Neurotoxins exert highly specific effects on the nervous system and tend to act rapidly. Some nerve toxins produce symptoms similar to chemical nerve agents. These agents overload nerve paths; cause loss of coordination, pinpointing of pupils, and convulsions; and lead to rigid paralysis. Other neurotoxins block the transmission of impulses along nerve and muscle fibers. Symptoms of these toxins include numbness (tingling) or weakness, tremors, and loss of muscular coordination that leads to severe muscle weakness and limp paralysis. Confusion, headache, blurred vision, and light sensitivity (due to dilation of pupils) can occur.

Cytotoxins

Cytotoxins cause cellular destruction or interfere with metabolic processes such as cell respiration or protein synthesis. Cytotoxins exert effects upon a variety of tissues and bodily systems (e.g., digestive, respiratory, circulatory). Symptoms of exposure may resemble those of vesicant (blister), vomiting, or choking chemical agents. Cytotoxin effects include irritation, blistering and lesions of the skin, nausea or vomiting, hemorrhaging, bloody diarrhea and vomit, difficulty in breathing, or sudden death.

Detection, Protection, and Decontamination

The nature and action of biological warfare agents make them particularly difficult to detect and identify. Intelligence reporting and overt dissemination are the best indications of a possible biological attack. Rapid field detection of biological warfare agents is not yet available. Samples must be sent to and evaluated at advanced laboratories. When employed during enemy operations, biological weapons can only be detected after significant numbers of unexplained sickness/death of personnel, animals, or plants occur. See FMFM 11-20, for specific guidance on field management of biological warfare agents.

Chemical Agents and Their Effects

Threat forces have many delivery systems capable of delivering chemical agents, including aircraft, rockets, field artillery, and mortars. Depending on the agent, these systems can deliver both persistent and nonpersistent agents by air burst or surface burst. Chemical agents are used to kill, injure, or incapacitate personnel. They are classified by their action and effects.

Effects produced by these agents are generally dose dependent (i.e., increased doses of a specific agent produce corresponding increases in the severity of its effects. The chemical warfare capabilities of threat nations dictate that U.S. forces be prepared to survive massive chemical attacks and continue to function effectively in a chemically-contaminated environment.

Chemical agents are classified by either their physiological action or their military use.

Nerve Agents

Nerve agents directly affect a person's nervous system and are highly toxic in both liquid and vapor forms. Whether absorbed through the skin or inhaled, the effects on the human body are the same. Vapor is readily absorbed by the eyes, nose, and throat tissue. Liquid readily penetrates the skin, eyes, and body tissue.

Blister Agents

Blister agents affect moist areas of the body. Eyes, respiratory tract, and sweating skin are particularly vulnerable. Some agents are painless upon initial contact; other agents may sting. Blister agents can range in color from colorless to dark brown oily liquid droplets but are typically an invisible vapor. Whether liquid or vapor, these agents burn or blister any internal or external part of the body that they contact. Inhaling blister agents causes serious damage to tissues in the mouth, nose, throat, and lungs. The degree of damage depends on the type and concentration of the agent, weather, an individual's physical activity, and exposure time. They are highly effective in minute quantities and often produce delayed casualties. Unprotected troops exposed to low vapor concentrations of a blister agent over an extended period of time will eventually become casualties.

Blood Agents

Blood agents are usually disseminated as vapors or gases and enter the body through respiration. These agents affect the circulatory and respiratory systems by blocking the blood's ability to deliver oxygen to body tissues. Symptoms range from dizziness (mild exposure) to convulsions and coma (high exposure). After inhaling a high concentration of a blood agent, a victim may become unconscious and die within a few minutes.

Choking Agents

Choking agents are usually disseminated as gases and enter the body through respiration. They affect the respiratory system by irritating or damaging lung tissue and, in extreme cases, cause the lungs to fill with fluid. These agents produce symptoms such as coughing, choking, tightness in the chest, nausea, headache, and watering of the eyes. Delayed effects usually occur within 2 to 4 hours (but can also occur up to 24 hours) after exposure and follow a period in which the individual experiences no initial effects. Delayed effects include rapid and shallow breathing, painful cough, discomfort and fatigue, shock, and frequently, death.

Incapacitant Agents

An incapacitant is a chemical agent that produces a temporary disabling condition that persists for hours to days after exposure. Medical treatment, while not essential, may decrease recovery time. Two groups of incapacitants exist: central nervous system (CNS) depressants and CNS stimulants. CNS depressants, such as the anticholinergic agent BZ, disrupt memory, problem solving, attention, and comprehension functions. High doses produce toxic delirium that destroys the ability to perform any military task. CNS stimulants, such as d-lysergic acid diethylamide (LSD), cause excessive nervous activity. Flooding the central nervous system with too much information makes concentration difficult and causes indecisiveness and an inability to act in a sustained, purposeful manner.

Riot Control Agents

Riot control agents are irritants with a very low toxicity level and a short duration of action. Little or no latent periods occur after exposure. Riot control agents cause excessive tearing, choking and coughing, and nausea and vomiting; higher exposures can cause blisters. O-chlorobenzylidene malononitrile (CS) is the most commonly used irritant for riot control purposes. Chloroacetophenone (CN) is used in some countries even though it is highly toxic. Arsenical smoke has also been used on the battlefield. A new riot control agent is dibenz-(b,f)-1,4-oxazepine (CR), but very little experience with this agent exists.

(reverse blank)

Chemical Training Agents and Munitions

Training munitions are used during training to simulate a combat environment. Tactical principles must be followed as if actual agents were being deployed.

Safety

Never sacrifice safety to obtain realism when emulating an actual combat situation. Review and analyze each trainee's physical condition before exposing the trainee to chemical simulants. Chemical simulants must be used properly and safely. Take the following safety precautions:

- Identify personnel who have severe facial acne, a history of asthma, serious respiratory conditions, or cardiac conditions. Refer these personnel to medical representatives prior to their participation in training.
- Adhere to the same safety limits required for high-explosive munitions.
- Provide unlimited consumption of water.
- Allow only water to be consumed through the drinking device of the field protective mask.

Authorized NBC Munitions and Agents

When planning an NBC defense training program, refer to special allowance listings to determine unit munition authorization; the allowance is different for each unit. The following partial list of munitions and agents authorized for training represents those that are commonly used in unit NBC training:

- Capsule, CS (used in mask confidence exercise).
- Grenade, hand, riot, CS (M-7A3 and M-25A2 types).
- Grenade, hand, smoke, high concentration.
- Grenade, hand, smoke (green, red, yellow, violet).
- Mine, land, 1-gallon, empty, chemical.
- Pot, smoke, large, 30-pound, high concentration.
- Irritant agent, CS1 and CS2.
- Cord, detonating (fuse primacord) pentaerythritoltetranitrate (PETN) (used with mines).
- Cap, blasting, electric, special.
- Simulator, atomic-explosion, M-142.
- Simulator, boobytrap (flash, illumination, and whistles).
- Simulator, hand grenade.
- Simulator, projectile, ground burst.

Notes

The Threat

1. Robert S. McNamara as quoted in Robert Debs Heinl, Jr., Col, USMC, Retired, *Dictionary of Military and Naval Quotations* (Annapolis, MD: United States Naval Institute, 1966) p. 215.

2. Defense Intelligence Reference Document, MCIA-1586-001-97, *Marine Corps Midrange Threat Estimate—1997–2007: Finding Order in Chaos (U)* (Quantico, VA: Marine Corps Intelligence Activity, 3 September 1997) p. 61.

Organization and Responsibilities

1. Lieutenant General Hunter Liggett, USA, as quoted in Heinl, p. 308.

Combat Service Support in an NBC Environment

1. Maurice de Saxe as quoted in Heinl, p. 316.

Passive and Active NBC Planning Measures

1. Napoleon I as quoted in Heinl, p. 239.

NBC Defense Training

1. Douglas MacArthur as quoted in Heinl, p. 329.

Glossary

Section I. Abbreviations and Acronyms

ACE .... aviation combat element
AFJMAN .... Air Force joint manual
ATP .... allied tactical publication

BAS .... battalion aid station
BRM .... bioregulators/modulators

CBIRF .... Chemical/Biological Incident
Response Force
CN .... chloroacetophenone
CNS .... central nervous system
COC .... combat operations center
CR .... dibenz-(b,f)-1,4-oxazepine
CRTS .... casualty receiving and treatment ship
CS .... O-chlorobenzylidene malononitrile
CSS .... combat service support
CSSE .... combat service support element

e.g. .... for example
EPW .... enemy prisoner of war

FM .... U.S. Army field manual
FMFM .... Fleet Marine Force manual
FSCC .... fire support coordination center
FSSG .... force service support group

GCE .... ground combat element

H&S .... headquarters and service
HSS .... health service support

i.e.,...that is
IPB .... intelligence preparation of the battlespace/battlefield
ITS .... individual training standard

JINTACCS.................... Joint Interoperability Tactical Command
and Control Systems

LSD.. d-lysergic acid diethylamide

MAG .... Marine aircraft group
MAGTF .... Marine air-ground task force
MAW .... Marine aircraft wing
MCIA.................................... Marine Corps Intelligence Activity
MCO .... Marine Corps order
MCWP .... Marine Corps warfighting publication
METT-T ....mission, enemy, terrain and weather, troops
and support available-time available
MEU..Marine expeditionary unit
MOPP......................................mission-oriented protective posture
MOS... military occupational specialty
MWSS.. Marine wing support squadron

NAPP ....nerve agent pyridostigmine pretreatment
NAVMED .... naval medical
NBC ....nuclear, biological, and chemical
NBCD .... nuclear, biological, and chemical detachment
NBC ESU................................NBC equipment surveillance unit
NCO ....noncommissioned officer

OPCON .... operational control

PETN ....pentaerythritoltetranitrate
POW...prisoners of war

QSTAG...........................quadripartite standardization agreement

SOP .... standing operating procedures
STANAG .... standardization agreement

TAMCN .... table of authorized material control number
TRAP .... tactical recovery of aircraft and personnel
T/E .... table of equipment
T/O .... table of organization

U.S. .... United States

WMD .... weapon of mass destruction

Section II. Definitions

The following terms are used in the description and application of NBC doctrine, tactics, techniques, and procedures, and the organizational structure of NBC units.

B

biological agent—(DOD, NATO) A microorganism that causes disease in personnel, plants, or animals or causes the deterioration of materiel. (Joint Pub 1-02)

biological defense—(DOD, NATO) The methods, plans, and procedures involved in establishing and executing defensive measures against attacks using biological agents. (Joint Pub 1-02)

biological weapon—(DOD, NATO) An item of materiel which projects, disperses, or disseminates a biological agent including arthropod vectors. (Joint Pub 1-02)

blast—(DOD, NATO) The brief and rapid movement of air, vapor or fluid away from a center of outward pressure, as in an explosion or in the combustion of rocket fuel; the pressure accompanying this movement. This term is commonly used for "explosion," but the two terms may be distinguished. (Joint Pub 1-02)

blast wave—(DOD) A sharply defined wave of increased pressure rapidly propagated through a surrounding medium from a center of detonation or similar disturbance. (Joint Pub 1-02)

blister agent—(DOD, NATO) A chemical agent that injures the eyes and lungs, and burns or blisters the skin. Also called **vesicant agent**. (Joint Pub 1-02)

blood agent—(DOD, NATO) A chemical compound, including the cyanide group, that affects bodily functions by preventing the normal utilization of oxygen by body tissues. (Joint Pub 1-02)

C

chemical agent—(DOD, NATO) A chemical substance which is intended for use in military operations to kill, seriously injure, or incapacitate personnel through its physiological effects. The term excludes riot control agents, herbicides, smoke, and flame. (Joint Pub 1-02)

chemical defense—(DOD, NATO) The methods, plans and procedures involved in establishing and executing defensive measures against attack utilizing chemical agents. (Joint Pub 1-02)

chemical survey—(DOD, NATO) The directed effort to determine the nature and degree of chemical hazard in an area and to delineate the perimeter of the hazard area. (Joint Pub 1-02)

chemical warfare—(DOD) All aspects of military operations involving the employment of lethal and incapacitating munitions/agents and the warning and protective measures associated with such offensive operations. (This definition should be taken as to U.S. policy for employment of chemical agents. Policy is that the U.S. will not employ chemical agents. Riot control agents do not fall under this policy.) Since riot control agents and herbicides are not considered to be chemical warfare agents, those two items will be referred to separately or under the broader term "chemical", which will be used to include all types of chemical munitions/agents collectively. The term "chemical warfare weapons" may be used when it is desired to reflect both lethal and incapacitating munitions/agents of either chemical or biological origin. (Joint Pub 1-02)

choking agents—This class of agents includes chlorine and phosgene, both of which were used in World War I. In sufficient concentrations, their corrosive effect on the respiratory system results in pulmonary edema, filling the lungs with fluid and choking the victim.

contamination—(DOD) 1. The deposit, absorption, or adsorption of radioactive material, or of biological or chemical agents on or by structures, areas, personnel, or objects. 2. Food and/or water made unfit for consumption by humans or animals because of the presence of environmental chemicals, radioactive elements, bacteria or organisms, the byproduct of the growth of bacteria or organisms, the decomposing material (to include the food substance itself), or waste in the food or water. (Joint Pub 1-02)

contamination control—(DOD, NATO) Procedures to avoid, reduce, remove, or render harmless, temporarily or permanently, nuclear, biological, and chemical contamination for the purpose of maintaining or enhancing the efficient conduct of military operations. (Joint Pub 1-02)

D

decontamination—(DOD, NATO) The process of making any person, object, or area safe by absorbing, destroying, neutralizing, making harmless, or removing chemical or biological agents, or by removing radioactive material clinging to or around it. (Joint Pub 1-02)

decontamination station—(DOD, NATO) A building or location suitably equipped and organized where personnel and materiel are cleansed of chemical, biological, or radiological contaminants. (Joint Pub 1-02)

E

electromagnetic pulse—(DOD) The electromagnetic radiation from a nuclear explosion caused by Compton-recoil electrons and photoelectrons from photons scattered in the materials of the nuclear device or in a surrounding medium. The resulting electric and magnetic fields may couple with electrical/electronic systems to produce damaging current and voltage surges. May also be caused by nonnuclear means. Also called **EMP**. (Joint Pub 1-02)

F

fallout—(DOD, NATO) The precipitation to Earth of radioactive particulate matter from a nuclear cloud; also applied to the particulate matter itself. (Joint Pub 1-02)

fallout prediction—(DOD) An estimate, made before and immediately after a nuclear detonation, of the location and intensity of militarily significant quantities of radioactive fallout. (Joint Pub 1-02)

G

ground zero—(DOD, NATO) The point on the surface of the Earth at, or vertically below or above, the center of a planned or actual nuclear detonation. (Joint Pub 1-02)

I

incapacitating agent—(DOD) An agent that produces temporary physiological or mental effects, or both, which will render individuals incapable of concerted effort in the performance of their assigned duties. (Joint Pub 1-02)

incapacitating agent—(NATO) A chemical agent which produces temporary disabling conditions which (unlike those caused by riot control agents) can be physical or mental and persist for hours or days after exposure to the agent has ceased. Medical treatment, while not usually required, facilitates a more rapid recovery. See also **chemical agent; riot control agent.** (Joint Pub 1-02)

M

mycotoxin—A fungal or bacterial toxin (e.g., "yellow rain").

N

NBC defense—(DOD) Nuclear defense, biological defense, and chemical defense, collectively. The term may not be used in the context of US offensive operations. (Joint Pub 1-02)

nerve agent—(DOD, NATO) A potentially lethal chemical agent which interferes with the transmission of nerve impulses. (Joint Pub 1-02)

nuclear nation—(DOD, NATO) Military nuclear powers and civil nuclear powers. See also **nuclear power.** (Joint Pub 1-02)

nuclear power—(DOD, NATO) Not to be used without appropriate modifier. (Joint Pub 1-02)

nuclear radiation—(DOD, NATO) Particulate and electromagnetic radiation emitted from atomic nuclei in various nuclear processes. The important nuclear radiations, from the weapon standpoint, are alpha and beta particles, gamma rays, and neutrons. All nuclear radiations are ionizing radiations, but the reverse is not true; X-rays for example, are included among ionizing radiations, but they are not nuclear radiations since they do not originate from atomic nuclei. (Joint Pub 1-02)

nuclear weapon—**(DOD, NATO)** A complete assembly (i.e., implosion type, gun type, or thermonuclear type), in its intended ultimate configuration which, upon completion of the prescribed arming, fusing, and firing sequence, is capable of producing the intended nuclear reaction and release of energy. (Joint Pub 1-02)

R

residual radiation—**(DOD, NATO)** Nuclear radiation caused by fallout, artificial dispersion of radioactive material, or irradiation which results from a nuclear explosion and persists longer than one minute after burst. See also **contamination.** (Joint Pub 1-02)

riot control agent—**(DOD, NATO)** A substance which produces temporary irritating or disabling physical effects that disappear within minutes of removal from exposure. There is no significant risk of permanent injury, and medical treatment is rarely required. See also **incapacitating agent.** (Joint Pub 1-02)

T

thermal radiation—**(DOD, NATO)** 1. The heat and light produced by a nuclear explosion. (DOD) 2. Electromagnetic radiations emitted from a heat or light source as a consequence of its temperature; it consists essentially of ultraviolet, visible, and infrared radiations. (Joint Pub 1-02)

troop safety (nuclear)—**(DOD)** An element which defines a distance from the proposed burst location beyond which personnel meeting the criteria described under degree of risk will be safe to the degree prescribed. (Joint Pub 1-02)

Y

yield—See **nuclear yields.** (Joint Pub 1-02)

References and Related Publications

Allied Tactical Publication (ATP)

45   Reporting Nuclear Detonations, Biological and Chemical Attacks, and Predicting and Warning of Associated Hazards and Hazard Areas

Joint Publication (Joint Pub)

3-11   Joint Doctrine for Nuclear, Biological, and Chemical (NBC) Defense

Marine Corps Intelligence Activity Publication (MCIA)

1586-001-97   Marine Corps Midrange Threat Estimate—1997–2007: Finding Order in Chaos (U)

Marine Corps Orders (MCOs)

P1200.7R   Military Occupational Specialties Manual

1510.71A   Individual Training Standards (ITS) System for NBC Defense Specialists MOS 5711; and for NBC Officers, MOS 5702

3400.3   Nuclear, Biological, and Chemical (NBC) Defense Training

3960.5

Nuclear, Biological, and Chemical (NBC) Defense Equipment Test and Evaluation Program

Marine Corps Technical Instruction (TI)

10010-20/5

Serviceability Standards: Nuclear, Biological, and Chemical Defense Property

U.S. Army Field Manuals (FMs)

3-3/FMFM 11-17

Chemical and Biological Contamination Avoidance

3-3-1/FMFM 11-18

Nuclear Contamination Avoidance

3-4/FMFM 11-9

NBC Protection

3-5/FMFM 11-10

NBC Decontamination

3-6/AFM 105-7

Field Behavior of NBC Agents (Including Smoke and Incendiaries)

3-7/MCRP 3-37A

NBC Field Handbook

3-9/AFR 355-7

Potential Military Chemical/Biological Agents and Compounds

3-11/MCRP 3-3.7.2

Flame, Riot Control Agents and Herbicide Operations

3-14/MCRP 3-37.1A

Nuclear, Biological, and Chemical (NBC) Vulnerability Analysis

3-19/FMFM 11-20

NBC Reconnaissance

3-21

Chemical Accident Contamination Control

3-100/MCWP 3-3.7.1

Chemical Operations, Principles, and Fundamentals

8-285/
NAVMED P-5041/
AFJMAN 44-149/
FMFM 11-11

Treatment of Chemical Agent Casualties
and Conventional Military Chemical Injuries

U.S. Army Technical Manuals (TMs)

3-216/AFM 355-6

Technical Aspects of Biological Defense

3-4230-204-12&P

Operator's and Unit Maintenance Manual (Including Repair Parts and Special
Tools List) for Decontaminating Apparatus, Portable, DS2, 1 1/2 Quart, ABC-M11
(NSN 4230-00-720-1618)

3-4230-216-10

Operator's Manual for Decontaminating
Kit, Skin: M258A1 (NSN 4230-01-101-
3984) and Training Aid, Skin Decontaminating: M58A1 (6910-01-101-1768)

3-4230-228-10

Operator's Manual for Decontaminating
Apparatus: Power-driven, Lightweight,
M17 (NSN 4230-01-251-8702)

3-6665-307-10

Operators Manual for Chemical Agent
Detector Kit, M256 (NSN 6665-01-016-
8399) and M256A1 (6665-01-133-4964)

11-6665-232-20P

Organizational Maintenance Repair Parts
and Special Tools List for Radiacmeters,
IM-174A/P (NSN 6665-00-999-5145)
and IM-174B/PD (6665-01-056-7422)

11-6665-236-12

Operator's and Organizational Maintenance Manual for Radiac Set, AN/PDR-
75 (NSN 6665-01-211-4217)

11-6665-251-10

Operator's Manual for Radiac Set AN/
VDR-2 (NSN 6665-01-222-1425)

International Standardization Agreements
North Atlantic Treaty Organization Agreements
(STANAGs)

2002	Warning Signs For The Marking of Contaminated or Dangerous Land Areas, Complete Equipments, Supplies and Stores.
2047	Emergency Alarms of Hazard or Attack (NBC And Air Attack Only)
2083	Commander's Guide on Nuclear Radiation Exposure of Groups
2103	Reporting Nuclear Detonations, Biological and Chemical Attacks and Predicting and Warning of Associated Hazards and Hazards Areas—ATP–45(A)
2104	Friendly Nuclear Strike Warning
2112	NBC Reconnaissance
2133	Vulnerability Assessment of Chemical and Biological Hazards
2150	NATO Standards of Proficiency for NBC Defence
2352	NBC Defense Equipment Operational Guidelines
2353	Evaluation of NBC Defense Capability
2358	First Aid and Hygiene Training in NBC Operations
2412	The Effects of Wearing Individual Protection Equipment on Individual and Unit Performance During Exercises—AXP-8

2426	NBC Contamination Control Policy for NATO Forces
2429	Personnel Identification While in NBC Individual Protective Equipment
2451	Doctrine for the NBC Defense of NATO Forces
2500	NATO Handbook on the Medical Aspects of NBC Defensive Operations—AMedP–6(A)
2871	First-Aid Materiel for Chemical Injuries
2873	Concept of Operations of Medical Support in Nuclear, Biological and Chemical Environments—AMedP–7(A)
2910	Nuclear Casualty and Damage Assessment for Exercises—AXP-6
2917	Chemical Casualty Assessment Exercise Publication—AXP-7(A)
2941	Guidelines for Air and Ground Personnel Using Fixed and Transportable Collective Protection Facilities on Land
2954	Training of Medical Personnel for NBC Operations
2984	Graduated Levels of NBC Threat and Associated Protection

American, British, and Canadian Agreements
Quadripartite Standardized Agreements (QSTAGs)

183	Emergency Warning Signals and Alarms for NBC Hazards or Attacks

187   Reporting Nuclear Detonations, Radio-active Fallout, and Biological and Chemical Attacks and Predicting Associated Hazards and Hazard Areas

189   Friendly Nuclear Strike Warning (Based on STANAG 2104)

207   Calculator Set, Nuclear M-28A1

244   Nuclear Hardening Criteria for Military Equipment

283   Area Predictor, Radiological Fallout, M-5A2

446   Simulator, Projectile, Airburst, Liquid Chemical Agent L1A2 (SPAL)

465   Guidelines For Commanders in Coping with Operational Problems Associated with Miosis

495   Riot Control and Training Agents CS and CR

496   Standards for NBC Protective Mask and Canister Screw Threads

608   Detector Kits Chemical Agent US-M256, M256A1 and Training Tickets (M256) UK–Residual Vapour, No. 1 Mk 1 and Tactical Training Aid. No. 1 Mk 1, CA-C2 and Training Kit

620   Consistent Set of Nuclear Hardening Criteria for Communications Electronics (C-E) Equipment

651   Paper, Chemical Agent Detector

2000   Guidelines on Entry and Exit Procedures for Using Collective Protection Facilities

2003   ABCA Reference Publication on National Individual NBC Protection

www.ingramcontent.com/pod-product-compliance
Lightning Source LLC
Chambersburg PA
CBHW070537290526
45790CB00002B/530